Leabharlanna Poiblí Chathair Baile Átha Cliath

Dublin City Public Libraries

ADVANTAGE

LESSONS FROM SPORT AND BUSINESS TO ACHIEVE YOUR GOALS

JAMES CLUSKEY

Dublin City Public Libraries

Advantage

First published in 2020 by

Panoma Press Ltd
48 St Vincent Drive, St Albans, Herts, AL1 5SJ, UK
info@panomapress.com
www.panomapress.com

Book layout by Neil Coe.

978-1-784529-13-0

The right of James Cluskey to be identified as the author of this work has been asserted in accordance with sections 77 and 78 of the Copyright, Designs and Patents Act 1988.

A CIP catalogue record for this book is available from the British Library.

All rights reserved. No part of this book may be reproduced in any material form (including photocopying or storing in any medium by electronic means and whether or not transiently or incidentally to some other use of this publication) without the written permission of the copyright holder except in accordance with the provisions of the Copyright, Designs and Patents Act 1988. Applications for the copyright holder's written permission to reproduce any part of this publication should be addressed to the publishers.

This book is available online and in bookstores.

Copyright 2020 James Cluskey

ACKNOWLEDGEMENTS

Thank you to everyone who made this possible. Thanks to Mindy for taking me through the process and everyone at Panoma Press for working with me and believing in this book.

This book is dedicated to everyone who has supported me throughout my journey from being a shy boy who started in Parks Tennis to go on and represent my country in Davis Cup, play professional tennis and hold a Guinness World Record.

To all the people who helped me make the transition from sport into business, and who have guided and are still guiding me along the way.

Special note to my parents Kevin and Esme and my brother Stephen and sister Amy. Thank you for making me who I am today and for always supporting me.

Thanks to the test readers Amy Brand, Ed Brand, Greg Rose and Fabio Molle.

Thanks to the stars of the book, including a few who I have not yet met, for giving me the opportunity to share the lessons I learned from them.

David Mullins, Dan O'Neill, Luke Maguire, Sir Richard Branson, Leo Daniel Ryan, Conor Niland, Kevin Clancy, Gary Cahill, Sam Barry, Larry Jurovich, Stephen Twadell, Daragh Sheridan, David McKernan, Pat Lam, Ray Nolan, Ken Skupski, Louis Cayer, Paul Hanley, Dr Betty Uribe, Robin Sharma, Aidan Moran, Max Mirnyi, John Morrissey, Daniel Glancy, David O'Hare, Peter Clarke, John Connor, Paul O'Connell, Dan Kiely, Linda Kiely, Jeff Brown, Malcom Gladwell, Tim Gannon, Kurt Long, Teresa Long, James McGee, Karol Beck, Magnus Gustafsson, Alan Temple, Tonya Lanthier, Owen Casey, Stephen Cluskey, Val Quinn, Purav Raja, Mahesh Bhupathi, Rohan Bopanna, Crystal Sacca, Chris Sacca, Michael Venus, Freddy Nielsen, Jonathan Marray, Ed Brand, Sania Mirza, Ciara Mageen, Paul Salem, Peter Silvester, Johnny Barr, Dan Grossman, Cathy Grossman, Padraig Harrington, Brian Chesky, Eric Cantona, Ray Dalio, Ashley Tatum, Fabrice Martin, Conor Taylor.

CONTENTS

INTRODUCTION

Many people have asked me why I've decided to write this book. If I'm brutally honest I've always wanted to write a book. I love to read, especially when travelling. The moment came when I was on an early Dublin to London flight reading the very good entrepreneur Sean Gallagher's book *Secrets to Success* where he details the lessons learned from great Irish entrepreneurs that I thought it's time for me to write a book and share my own learnings from the incredible business people and sportspeople I've met from around the world.

Also as we move further through life our memories and stories become a little fuzzy. I wanted to capture these learnings so that I wouldn't forget them and that I can call on them during hard times to help motivate myself and remember that inspiration.

I started tennis at six years old in the Parks Tennis programme. I was a shy boy and my mum encouraged me to play. I get goosebumps thinking about coming from a club with a portacabin and six tarmac courts to where my tennis has taken me and what the sport has given me along the way. It's an incredibly challenging and difficult sport but it has taken me to places I can only dream of. Through tennis I've got to see the world from going on a sports scholarship to play college tennis at Louisiana State University, to playing professional tournaments in every corner of the globe, playing Davis Cup for Ireland and breaking a Guinness World Record for the longest doubles tennis match for charity.

I have been lucky enough to meet some amazing people throughout my journey thus far and no doubt I will meet more amazing people in the future. Not everyone in life has been lucky enough to have the same privileges as me and I wanted to share my learnings from my own journey and from the people I've met.

I have met wonderful women throughout my journey in both personal life and in business, but I realised while writing the book the majority of my stories in the book are related to men. I spent most of my time being coached and mentored by men throughout my tennis and business journey. When the sequel comes out I will have more stories with the female leaders I have worked with.

Success for me with my book is that if the reader can take lessons or learnings into their business or personal life which helps them become successful in whatever that means for them. This is the type of book you can dip in and out of. You could be on a flight and read a few chapters and then a little time later you could dip back into it. This is the way I want it to be.

I feel I've had a unique journey coming from a non-tennis country like Ireland and making it to 145 in the world in doubles tennis and then going into starting my own business. I heard someone say how one conversation or phone call can change your life. Well a phone call with the co-founder of the Necker Cup, Trevor Short, did change my life. I have been lucky enough to spend time with one of the most well-known entrepreneurs in the world, Sir Richard Branson, and learning lessons from him while also then working in the corporate environment with businesses around high performance. I have been on both sides of the fence and tried to capture the lessons in the book.

Sometimes when we see a professional sportsperson talk about performance they don't understand the day to day challenges in corporate life of balancing everything. I have seen both sides and feel I'm able to relate to both sides on this issue. I hope that this book will have something for everyone no matter at what stage you are on your journey.

I have had successes in my journey but I have also had failures in both my professional and personal life including not making the Wimbledon Championships which I just missed out on. We are all fighting our own battles in our professional and personal life and hopefully this book will help you to push forward and help you in what you are looking to achieve.

This book is also for me. I wanted to capture my life so far and reflect on the successes and failures I've had. There have been a lot on both sides. All we can do is learn and try to take the learnings and keep moving forward.

With my business HC Collective I do one to one coaching with people around goal setting and performance, team programmes for corporates looking to work better together and hit targets, and also a lot of speaking on the topic of high performance, career transition and networking.

When it comes to high performance we apply the same tools to professional sport as business but tailor it specifically to business and help the individual or team succeed in what they are looking to achieve.

I would like you to read this book as a blueprint to help you attain your goals. Sit down and write the goals out and have a clear action plan to go and realise whatever it is you are looking to accomplish.

CHAPTER 1

CREATING A PLAN

It's easier to achieve with a detailed plan

In business, sport and life it's hard to do things without a plan. A lot of people both in business and personal life don't have a blueprint to follow. According to the best research, less than 3% of Americans have written goals, and less than 1% review and rewrite their goals on a daily basis. This blows my mind. People like milestones and key moments in time. I think that's why New Year's resolutions only last a certain number of days before they have bitten the dust. I read a report from the fitness app Strava that the majority of people's New Year's resolutions are given up on by 19 January.

I strongly believe you need a detailed plan at the start to help you navigate where you are trying to go. Note the word detailed – it's not just a few lines on a page. It's a clear blueprint that guides your journey. Everyone now uses Google Maps and sometimes we take the wrong turn and the map updates our direction. In goal setting the same rules apply. You may be off track at a moment in time but you need to be agile and readjust and maybe take a similar route to help you get there.

The plan will evolve and change

I always loved the quote from Mike Tyson: "Everyone has a plan until they get punched in the face." In my professional tennis career I always had a map of goals and ranking points I needed to achieve to hit my ranking goal. However, we need to be aware that things happen which are out of our control. You get injured, sick or have personal problems. This is OK but we need to understand and be comfortable with the fact that the plan could change and that's OK. I'm a big football fan and was never a good player but love watching it. I love the battles between the great managers, and when a manager sets out his game plan but then something happens – maybe you go a goal down or there is a sending off – the team needs to be OK with altering the plan and moving forward with it. Plans can change in the moment and you have to make a strong decision to change things when they are not going to plan in business, sport and life.

In 2017 I broke a Guinness World Record with three other players – David Mullins, Dan O'Neill and Luke Maguire. We played for 60 hours and 24 minutes and 19 seconds. I had finished my tennis career at the end of 2015 and actually wanted something to train for. I thought of doing a marathon, Ironman or something along those lines, but I never fully committed and I didn't think it was for me. While on the pro tennis tour a couple of Irish players had attempted to break the record. They had done 33 hours and they had to stop because one of the players got cramp. I remembered this and thought that's interesting. Then when I coached Sir Richard Branson on Necker in 2016 I was speaking to him about his ballooning world records and stories. You can sense his pride in them and I was inspired by them. His son Sam had just released the documentary *Don't Look Down* about Richard's record and I was further inspired by that.

I met Dave Mullins who was on the Irish Davis Cup team the generation before me and said, "What do you think of this record and could we do it for charity?" I have to be honest and say that if Dave had said no I'm not sure if I would have run off to find other people. Luckily Dave said yes and I spoke to Dan O'Neill, a good tennis player from my local club who I thought I could convince. He actually didn't need much convincing and was in straight away and Dave spoke to Luke Maguire who was part of the failed record attempt but wasn't the person that cramped and Dave thought he would be perfect for it. We then approached a charity called Enjoy Tennis run by Liam O'Donogue and the agreement was they would take care of the logistics like clocks, volunteers and raising money and we would take care of the training. We recruited a great trainer, Leo Daniel Ryan, who has broad knowledge around fitness, nutrition and breathing and he was extremely important to us breaking the record.

The rules of the record were you had a five-minute break per hour and you could accumulate that time, so if we played for four hours then we would have a 20-minute break. What we did was take 5 minutes and bank 15 minutes so that we could have an hour's sleep each night over the 60 hours. Dave created a great plan of where we would take our breaks etc. We started playing on Friday morning and finished on Sunday evening. We had that plan but it changed a few times. One time Mother Nature called and I needed to run to the toilet asap, and another time Dan was struggling and we needed to take an unexpected break. We had our plan but as a group we needed to be open to the fact that things can go wrong and to expect that.

In tennis I would have a set of tournaments I was going to play, which for example could be three low-level tournaments in France. However, if a spot opened up for whatever reason in a higher level tournament then I would go there instead. I may have mentally prepared to play in the UK but suddenly I was on a flight to France. I remember one instance on the tour where I arrived at Dublin Airport to fly to Germany for a tournament on the Saturday. I was about to check in for my flight to go to Germany and my doubles partner for the week Darren Walsh called me and said, "Can you get to France? The draw will be weaker here and we will be seeded." I said to hang on and it just so happened that Aer Lingus had a flight to Paris in a few hours and I flew there instead. Be open and OK with plans evolving.

A plan gives you confidence

When the plan is made it will give you that confidence to go and achieve. When I thought about playing for 60 hours for the Guinness World Record I thought wow this is going to be tough. I remember the moment Dave sent the Excel sheet with the plan for the record attempt. It sounds a little crazy but it did seem much easier. We knew we would have breaks at certain stages and I felt a surge of confidence. If we had started with the intent to play for 60 hours and had no idea when we were going to stop for breaks etc, we wouldn't have been able to do it.

We also had a plan in relation to our training, which gave us confidence. Leo Daniel Ryan had the group doing a lot of breathing work and training which I found hugely beneficial. If I'm honest I was sceptical at the start but I noticed it was making a difference and kept doing it. We were executing our strategy in the weeks leading up and it gave us the confidence to go and achieve the plan. One thing which I liked about Leo was that his plans were unique to the individual. In terms of our breathwork he saw where we were and gave us a plan depending on our situation. The same was true with the nutrition advice he gave us. Dave is vegan and Leo gave us each an individual plan based on the food we liked.

When I finished college in 2015 I came out on to the tour and started playing professionally. I felt if you equated my college level into the pro game then I should have been doing better but my results were OK. I can't actually remember the first meeting but Irish number 1 at the time, Conor Niland, was working with a sports psychologist from

Cork, Kevin Clancy. Kevin had no tennis background and worked in the GAA and with businesses around performance. It was my first real meeting with a sports psychologist and I was a little sceptical. Gary Cahill who was the technical director of Tennis Ireland said he was good and also Conor gave Kevin good reviews. You always need to be open to learning and I met Kevin for a coffee.

Kevin is a quiet, softly spoken and very interesting man. He had a huge impact on my mindset around my goals and what I was looking to achieve. I said to Kevin that my goal was to be inside 250 in the world. He said that's great and how many points did I need to do that? I think I roughly knew the answer to his question. He asked me to break down exactly the points I needed to make to be inside 250 in the doubles world rankings. He then asked me how many tournaments I played a year. I said I played 30 tournaments and the ATP take your best 18 which goes towards your world ranking. He then asked me a powerful question, "Well what's the reason for you putting so much pressure on yourself every week?" I was going to these events with a weight on my shoulder and wasn't playing free.

I designed a plan which I put on my wall at home with the points breakdown of the goal. I knew exactly what I needed to do. I knew how many second rounds, quarters, semis, finals and wins I needed to make in order to achieve my goal. Now every time I came home after a trip I'd be excited to go upstairs and tick off my goal. The 250 ranking didn't seem as far away and I knew what I had to do. Through the years I went further and set goals on how many serves, returns, volleys etc I needed to do in a training week. It's hard to explain how much I enjoyed getting that pen and ticking off my goal and the confidence I gained from that. I do the same in business today and I get the same satisfaction from it. It gives me the confidence to go and achieve. The little things will help you achieve that big goal.

One of my first goals in tennis was to play Davis Cup for Ireland which I was lucky enough to do for a number of years. I had lots of incredibly tough and exciting matches in Davis Cup and there was always something special about playing Davis Cup. I played for a number of captains and one was Gary Cahill. My first cap was in 2006 at the age of 19 and my last cap was in 2015. I noticed an evolution in the professionalism of the Irish team over the years and Gary was very professional and analytical. Sam Barry and I won our match against Egypt when we played against Sherif Sabry and Mohamad Safwat in straight sets 6-2 7-6 6-2.

Memories start to fade from specific matches as you get older but I do remember Gary had done a lot of research and video work on the guys and going into the match we had a detailed plan that we were confident in executing, and we did. We watched videos of them playing in the days leading up to the match and the plan gave me the confidence to achieve.

In 2020 with my company HC Collective I do a lot of offsites with companies helping the team to drive forward. There are a lot of similarities between performance in high-performance sport and business. One tech company I work with gave me some great insight. We created the plan in collaboration with the team. What one of the senior leaders said to me was, "Previously the sales target we have seemed like this impossible off in the distance number." It's very easy at the start of the year to set these huge sales targets and look at them and think great. However, the crucial thing is to create an execution plan to be able to go and do it.

You have an execution strategy

It's important to have an execution strategy. When you look at your goal you know what you have to achieve and understand the markers or blocks along the way. I got such pleasure in ticking off those points around my strategy. I would encourage you to use a physical pen to do this. It's OK to type your goals out but for me there's something great about using a physical pen to tick them off. I went one step further in that I changed some passwords to 'Iwillbe250' so that the goal was constantly on my mind. Now I'm not saying that you have to be that extreme but please write your goals out, own them and go after them.

I believe that as a sportsperson you can learn from business people and as a business person you can learn from sportspeople. A few years ago I very much enjoyed the documentary *Becoming Warren Buffett*. It's a story of someone who invested wisely and amassed a fortune of $80 billion most of which he's given away to the Bill and Melinda Gates Foundation. Just to be clear, I don't put money as the only indicator to success but I have the utmost respect for these business people. Bill Gates' father once asked both him and Warren to write down one word to describe their success. They both wrote down the same word: focus. They focused on achieving their goals, had a clear plan and execution strategy.

I do a lot of speaking on the topic of high performance in companies across industries. Sometimes I am advertised as a motivational speaker. I'm actually extremely uncomfortable with that term. I've been lucky enough to achieve goals but have also failed on a lot of goals too. In 2012 my ranking was about 150 in the lead-up to Wimbledon. I needed to have some decent results prior to the tournament to make the draw but I didn't and I missed the draw by one spot. I had an execution strategy and knew exactly what I needed to do but didn't get it done. It's still something I think about from time to time. As I reflect on my tennis career I think I moved away from the execution strategy and process and started thinking about the outcome. The former Irish rugby coach Joe Schmidt used to always say, "Focus on the process," and I lost sight of that. Please stick to that execution strategy.

My old coach Larry Jurovich introduced me as a 15-year-old to the legendary UCLA basketball coach John Wooden. Wooden is a legend of coaching. He was nicknamed the Wizard of Westwood; he won 10 national championships in a 12-year period as head coach of UCLA, including a record of seven in a row. No other team has won more than four in a row in Division 1 college men's or women's basketball. I always loved his definition of success which is: "Success is peace of mind which is a direct result in self-satisfaction in knowing you made the effort to be the best you can."

You have to do your absolute best whatever that is. You are not competing with anyone else except yourself. When Wooden was asked who was the most successful player he had coached he said that was a difficult question. Was it the guy who walked into UCLA with no scholarship and by year 4 was a serious contributor to the team, or was it the player who was amazing coming into the team and continued to be amazing?

I think about this around success and my tennis. Was I a successful tennis player? My ranking at 145 ATP is not amazing, however coming from a non-tennis background and a non-tennis country and all the factors around it I feel I did my absolute best and was at the ranking I should have reached. But was I good enough to play Wimbledon? Yes I was, and I think if I'd stayed focused on the execution strategy I would have achieved the goal, and it still stays with me.

You have something to reference

Tennis is an individual sport and in business sometimes you are in a team but more so an individual contributor to that team. It's great to have something to reference and look at. I had one copy of my plan in my room and one that was on my laptop with me. If I was in a hotel room around the world I would stare at the plan. As a business person I would encourage you to re-read your goals and look at them. It's one thing to set goals and never look at them for the rest of the year. You should reference them and check in with them.

You should make them visible and put them on your wall at home, on your bedroom mirror or your living room, or if they are work goals then put them there. Whatever works best for you but you absolutely need to see them. It brings a smile to my face thinking back to playing pro tennis and coming back after a trip and almost running up the stairs with a pen to tick them off. I would literally come back to Dublin Airport from a three-week trip and the first thing I would do would be go upstairs and tick my points off. I was moving one step closer.

I mentioned earlier the stat that only 3% of people write down their goals. Write your goals because to me it feels like you're making that commitment. Maybe they are written on a sheet of paper and beside your laptop in work, but the lesson is you need to see them and check in with them.

You must get an accountability partner

I'm a huge believer in an accountability partner. During my tennis career it was my tennis coach or psychologist. During my business career it's been an executive coach, mentor and girlfriend. I play a lot of tennis early in the morning. If I was going to the club to hit on the ball machine, then I might roll over in the morning a lot more than I do now. I think having someone external from your business is great too. I had Kevin the non-tennis sports psychologist. I found that beneficial in my career to have someone coming with a different approach. I do a lot of one to one executive coaching in organisations across industries. I think there is something powerful about someone external outside of the bubble challenging you on what's going on inside the bubble.

To keep you on track with your plan

You need someone that will challenge you on your plan and keep you on track when you veer off. If we use the Google Maps analogy again then maybe someone who will show you that similar route might actually be 20 minutes quicker. When I finished my playing career, I was unsure what I wanted to do. I signed up for a 10-week coaching programme which helps transitioning professional athletes. Did I find it useful? It was OK, it got me thinking of the future, but would I do it in hindsight? Probably not.

I coached a tennis clinic in Malahide. Stephen Twaddell, who is the former managing director of Kellogg's Europe and current chairman of several companies, investor and executive coach was there. I reached out through the tennis club and went and had a coffee with him. We have this unspoken agreement that I will coach him tennis and he will do some executive coaching with me. One coffee with him was better than the 10-week programme. He challenges me on my journey and gets me to think in different ways about what I am looking to achieve.

The only way someone is going to keep you on track with your plan is if you respect them. You have to be your own person, but at the same time I trust Stephen and have the utmost respect for him and his career. We don't need to meet every week but checking in to get him to ask probing questions around my plan has been hugely beneficial for me. Your accountability partner also needs to feel comfortable calling you out on your plan when it's not right. I do a lot of executive coaching and for the most part you're asking subtle questions whereas sometimes if needed and called for then that person needs to challenge you. Stephen has been great in terms of coaching/mentoring me and keeping me accountable.

Strength in numbers/someone in your corner

It is important to have someone in your corner pushing you on. You also need to have that mindset to drive yourself on. Tennis is a lonely sport and you spend a lot of time travelling on your own and being alone. I mentioned earlier changing my password to 'iwillbe250'. I have to keep myself accountable and push myself on to achieve. At the end of the day it's down to me how I show up and push myself on.

Somehow I came across the name Daragh Sheridan who worked as the head of capability and expertise at the Sport Ireland Institute. Daragh has since taken a role as the manager of High Performance Coaching in New Zealand and is a huge loss to Irish Sport. When I was going through my transition from pro sports into business I was introduced to Daragh as someone I should meet and have a coffee with. Daragh had a short career as a footballer and is one of the most impressive people I've come across.

Although I've only met him a handful of times he has had a huge impact on me. Daragh talked to me about career transition and as we ended the meeting and I shook his hand to say goodbye he said, "Strength in numbers." I agree with him fully. We need people in our corner who will push us and drive us on. It doesn't matter who it is but someone that can push us on and rein us in when we need that.

I am good friends with the founder of coffee company Java Republic, Dave McKernan. Dave is a really good man and has recently had a successful exit from the business. Dave has given me advice over the years and fancies himself as a bit of a tennis player. He is a good player and fierce competitor. He is an out and out entrepreneur. I interviewed Dave for one of my corporate events. Whether you meet Dave personally or in a business capacity he always talks about the people he has supporting him along the way. He always gives other people credit for his success. As a business person can you get a few business people together and meet for breakfast once a month and support each other but also challenge each other as well? I promise this will have a huge impact on your business if you can get that right cluster of people in the room.

People who tell you the truth

We all like to be told how good our idea is or how we appreciate feedback. The truth is it depends on the type of feedback. I spoke at a conference a few years ago where Pat Lam, who is a high-profile rugby coach who coached Connaught and is now at Bristol, was also a keynote speaker. The theme of the conference was taking the lessons from high-performance sport into business. Pat spoke about the concept of feedback. His point made the audience laugh but it really did make me think. He said when you speak to players and ask the question if they want feedback the answer is yes, but in reality is that really the case?

He told the story about bringing the team to dinner in Galway. One of the players asked for a steak and asked for it to be medium done. The steak came and the player made the comment that the steak was well done and he didn't like it but kept eating away. About five minutes into the group meal the manager approached the table and said the customary, "How's everyone's dinner tonight?" The player didn't say anything. Pat's point was he's doing himself a disservice but he's also doing the owner a disservice. That owner wants the feedback so that he can continue to improve the service. Seek people around you who will tell you the truth even if you don't like it. At least then you can make a decision.

Over the last few years I have become friends with Irish tech entrepreneur Ray Nolan. I got to know Ray through tennis and he has been a great mentor and friend to me. Ray was the founder of several companies including Hostelworld and xSellco. Ray is a tech guy and he is also the smartest guy in the room. I have asked Ray's advice on one or two things and the thing I like about him is you know you will get brutally honest feedback. OK sometimes it can be tough to take but you need people who are going to tell it like it is. It's good to hang around super positive people but I do think you need that friend or mentor who is well able to challenge your opinions and take you to task on them.

When I first started on the professional circuit in 2010 after college I went and played three future tournaments in Israel. For non-tennis people, futures are the lowest level of professional tournament. Ironically enough I didn't get into the first two tournaments and I got into the third tournament and won the doubles. It's not a life changer but I walked away from the tournament full of confidence. My old roommate in college and doubles partner Ken Skupski was in London working with Louis Cayer who is in my opinion the best doubles coach in the world. British doubles players have done amazingly well over the last few years and in my opinion a large reason for this is Louis.

I went to practise with these guys for a few days and again my eyes were opened. Ken and his then partner Colin Fleming were ranked 40 in the world and I was there as a practice partner. I hit this specific type of backhand return that I thought was good and helped me win at my level. One of the days I was told that Paul Hanley who was the number 5 in the world doubles player was going to come in and play with me against Ken and Colin. Louis pulled me aside that morning and said, "If you hit that doubles return playing with Paul Hanley he will walk off the court. That's a futures return." Now obviously Paul Hanley was not going to walk off the court. What Louis's feedback was that if you want to move to the next level you need to improve that return. Some people might take the huff and say what an arrogant man he is etc, but for me it was constructive feedback.

You must be clear on your vision

It sounds like such a simple thing. You need to know what you are trying to achieve in your personal life and work and go and achieve it. But it's easier said than done. You need to get clear on your vision.

Getting vision clarity

After a coaching stint I did on Necker Island with Richard Branson, I travelled to San Francisco to see a friend. I got a text from a friend in LA saying 'hey there is this business event on in two days' time and I have a spare ticket, would you like to come?'. I was essentially on holiday and said 'yeh why not' and I drove to LA. It was a 50-person event with people sitting around tables. I felt a little bit intimidated at the outset but I've always just thought go for it and try and keep my confidence up. Everyone has a story and in LA you meet so many interesting people.

There were speakers through the day and I started to relax until the host said, "Why don't we see who is in the room? Let's go around the room and introduce yourself, where you're from and what you do." This nervous feeling came over me but I got through that. I said, "Hey I'm James from Ireland, I'm a former pro tennis player who has just retired and I've just come from Necker where I coached Sir Richard Branson tennis."

At the end of the day people were networking. I would consider myself a good networker and I love meeting people but I didn't feel comfortable in this environment.

Then this small Colombian woman said, "Hey I'm Dr Betty Uribe, how are you?" Maybe she just saw this guy who stood out and didn't belong and she wanted me to feel comfortable. She said to me, "So what do you do?" I told her my story and she said, "What do you want to do now?" I said I didn't really know but I enjoy the people development space and might do some public speaking. She said, "Well I'm president of California Bank and I'm doing a bank offsite tomorrow morning for 100 employees. How would you like to come and speak to them?" I did everything to try and avoid it but she encouraged me and said, "I won't force you but am happy to coach you through."

The next morning I met her at 7am and she helped me prepare. I felt such a rush and after she came over and said, "Congratulations, you are now a keynote speaker for California Bank." We had a big hug and I thanked her. That's led to a friendship to this day and she has been an amazing mentor and supporter of mine. She wrote a book called *Values* which I would recommend reading, asking yourself the question: what's important to me? Companies have values, am I living them? What are my personal values?

I am 33 years old as I write this but have been lucky enough to spend time around some amazing sportspeople and business people. I look at some of them and I think it's about legacy. If you were having a coffee with yourself in 20 years' time what would you say to yourself? What do you want to be remembered by? This plays on my mind even now. Tennis wise I wanted to get to my highest possible ranking, play Davis Cup for Ireland, travel the world and play Wimbledon. I achieved most of that vision. What is your vision? And what do you want to achieve?

I read an article about Bill Gates once where he discussed taking a reading holiday. I thought wow this is incredibly interesting. I go on reading surges where I get really into books but then I fall away and go and watch keynotes. It's important to be constantly learning but it's also crucial to have some alone time.

In 2016 I had to go on a work trip on my own and stayed in a hotel in the middle of Ireland. I had to meet two people but other than that had complete 'me time'. At the time my mum said, "How will you get over the boredom?" I actually never saw it like that. I used to travel alone a lot as a tennis player and I actually missed that. I think it's important to carve out some 'me time'. I don't have kids so you might say that's easy for you to say, but can you find even 10-20 minutes in the day to have quiet time and reflect? This can help you to get clarity on your vision.

Get other people to buy into your vision

Don't be afraid to tell people your vision. If they believe in it then you will feed off it and get excited about it. You have to believe in it because if you don't then no one else will. How do you believe in your vision? When you get vision clarity of what you are trying to achieve then I think you can start to believe in it. In my pro tennis days when I broke my vision down it helped me buy into my vision.

You need to be enthusiastic about your vision. I have been hearing lots of startup business pitches over the last few years. Since I've been coaching Richard Branson tennis, people naturally bring me their business idea to get in front of him. One thing that strikes me is if the founder is not enthusiastic about the business in his pitch then how would you expect anyone else to be? With your team in work the leader must be enthusiastic about where things are going. I'm not saying the CEO has to be jumping up and down, everyone has their own personality, but you must have this air of optimism with your team to get them going in the right direction.

I'm very lucky that my parents, especially my mum, supported my tennis from an early age. I think through my passion, work rate and enthusiasm for the sport they wanted me to continue to get better. My mum believed in my vision for tennis and wanted me to be happy. She would be the first person I'd message after a great win or bad loss and she always encouraged me to keep going. She didn't say the right things 100% of the time but was always in my corner. I remember after a bad loss she would text and say 'keep going, things will turn around'. I'm lucky to inherit that positive attitude. However, I do think she believed in my vision because through my dedication she bought into it.

You must have your own vision

I became obsessed with achieving my goals. However, they were my goals and not someone else's. Too many times in business and sport you meet people who are living someone else's goals. This is common in tennis where pushy parents push their children along. For every player that makes it there is a significant number that end up hating the sport and simply burn out. There is a fine line between encouraging and pushing your kids. You must create your own vision and what you are looking to achieve. This is also common in corporate life. There are people who are lawyers or doctors because that's what their parents either did or wanted them to do. Follow your own path and create your own vision around it.

When I retired from professional tennis at the end of 2015 I didn't have a clear idea of what I wanted to do. I'm a social person and I started meeting people and asking their advice. Now you will hear me talk a lot around the power of having a coach, mentor etc. I also find sometimes that you can get too much advice and have to make your own decisions in life too. I have since worked with a lot of athletes transitioning out of sport and business people transitioning into industries or roles. Everyone will tell you that you should be doing this and that but it all depends on what you want to do. In hindsight I actually think I met too many people. I would suggest meeting a few people but in the end it's your vision so go and do it. You are the one that has to get up in the morning and live your vision.

CHAPTER 2

TAKING A STEP BACK

You need to slow down

Life goes by fast and people are busy being busy. In corporate life sometimes I find there are meetings about meetings and you just need to slow down and take a step back to go forward. Maybe sometimes I've fallen victim to being too relentless on a goal and losing sight of what I have in terms of my personal relationships. All you can do is learn from this and try to move forward.

Pressure causes people to speed up

In the 2002 World Cup Ireland had a good football team. We headed to the World Cup full of hope for a good run. During the build-up our best player and captain Roy Keane was sent home, or left, depending who you talk to, after fighting with the Ireland manager Mick McCarthy.

Public opinion was split down the middle on who to support. The fans got behind the team and we made it through to the last 16 where we played Spain. It was one of the most amazing matches I've ever seen and we should have won on the night but ended up losing on penalties. Our penalties were terrible and we lost the shootout only scoring two.

As a football fan I bought the DVD which reviewed Ireland's performances. Aidan Moran who is a professor and sports psychologist looked at the penalty shootout. He made the point that pressure causes people to speed up because they want to get out of the situation as quickly as possible. He asked the viewer to note how rushed and stressed the players looked. They simply needed to slow down and take their time. With goal setting you need to take that step back to get clarity so you can push forward as opposed to rushing into it. Pressure makes us rush.

In 2014 we played away to Belarus in Davis Cup. This was one of the most special moments of my life. The first time I ever went to watch a Davis Cup match was in 1997 when I was 11 years old and Ireland played Belarus, and the Belarusian player Max Mirnyi was my hero. I got his autograph that day and hung it proudly on my wall. Mirnyi went on to have a career high ranking of 18 in the world in singles and the number 1 doubles player in the world winning 10 doubles and mixed grand slams. He also won an Olympic Gold mixed doubles medal beating Andy Murray and Laura Robson in the London 2012 Olympics with Victoria Azerenka. He was an absolute hero of mine.

When we played them that year he was still ranked top 30 in the world but had headed into the twilight of his career.

I've been on the Davis Cup team since 2006 but this was one of the funniest ties we ever had. As a team we didn't stand much of a chance. We were missing our top singles players and John Morrisey who played college at Stanford and Daniel Glancy both lost singles as expected. They fought hard but just weren't good enough. Dave O'Hare and I were due to play doubles against Mirnyi and Aliaksandr Bury. Mirnyi is 6ft 6 and nicknamed 'The Beast' and he was playing with Bury who is 6ft 9 and was ranked 59 in the world in doubles. Bury was a nice guy and I used to call him 'The Monster'. It didn't help that Dave was coming from Memphis and his rackets hadn't arrived. We only got them two days before the match. Dave was a great player and a really good man. He's very athletic and good around the net and is very talented.

We had no real pressure going into the match and played amazingly well. I was on fire and feeling really good. I just had one major issue and that was my serve. I'm not sure what was going on but I was nervous on it. I couldn't relax. I needed to slow down and breathe. We managed to keep it together but ended up losing; after having match point in the fourth set we lost in the fifth set. We lost the match 7-6 6-7 7-5 6-7 2-6 and I was gutted but proud. I do miss those moments in the heat of battle. I regret not slowing down on my serve and not being able to control my thoughts. I needed to step out of the situation and step back in. If you're struggling with something in your personal life or in business then take that moment to slow down and regroup.

Pressure does strange things to people and we need to acknowledge it, learn from it and move forward with it. I always think of my mum travelling through the airport. There's that moment where she panics wondering where her passport is or where her gate is. She is so flustered she can't make a decision. Try not to let pressure speed you up too much.

I believe in the power of breathwork in performance

This is something I wish I'd understood more in my tennis career. The techniques would have helped me in that Belarus match. We have said for years, "Oh take a deep breath" or "relax" etc but we have never gone too deep into it. In the last few years since my debut with California Bank I've been doing some speaking in front of small and large crowds. One of the biggest fears people have is public speaking. It's terrifying for people. I remember a speaker said to me before my first Irish presentation, "You won't believe how much you will sweat during that first talk." It's true and although the nerves are getting a little easier I still get nervous. I've started doing breathwork before every talk and it's really helped me. I literally find the nearest toilets and before every talk I look in the mirror and take 10 deep breaths, inhale exhale, while looking in the mirror. I've found that it helps me focus and get in the right state to speak. If you have a presentation or an important interview or something of significance, take a few minutes to slow down and focus on your breathing beforehand.

Meditation

I believe in the power of meditation when it comes to performance and love all these apps out there that support people with this journey. However, I have to be honest and say that I've struggled to meditate and still feel my mind wander. I've started using Headspace which has helped me and I do feel I'm improving my levels of focus. I know and believe meditation works but so far I haven't been able to find my happy place with it. I'd encourage you to find what works for you but do focus on your breathing.

Breathwork with Leo

In the months leading up to the Guinness World Record I said to Dave that we needed a trainer/fitness coach/ nutritionist and preferably all of those things in one. Initially someone introduced us to a trainer but he had no interest in us and that was clear. I had met Leo through the gym I trained in as a pro tennis player. He is a positive, fun and genuine person. I had fallen out of contact with Leo but when I explained the situation to my friend he suggested reaching out to him.

I called Leo and I have to say in terms of the world record it was the best thing I ever did. He is so passionate about supporting people it's contagious. He helped us with everything and we can't thank him enough. One interesting thing about him is he ran the Dublin marathon with his mouth taped closed. He believes in the power of the breath and did a session with us. I was sceptical at first but I did the exercises and I can say that during the world record the breathing exercises helped us slow down, relax and find a good place. I have continued to do these exercises on a daily basis and I find that taking a step back in a stressful situation and focusing on your breathing can really help you move forward.

Celebrate your victories

You need to celebrate those small victories along the way. In Ireland celebrating can mean going out to have 10 pints of beer but I don't mean it like that. I remember when we beat Estonia in Davis Cup our number 1 singles player Conor Niland said we need to go and celebrate. He was absolutely right. His point was at the end of your career what will you remember? You will remember these moments and times and that you should celebrate them. Now that I've stopped playing for a few years I do miss those moments, but I can still have them now and celebrate if I land a client or a talk goes very well.

In corporate life if you and your team achieve a milestone then celebrate. I facilitate lots of offsites for companies and one of the powers of them is getting people together to celebrate and then go again. I want to be crystal clear that it doesn't have to be alcohol related but life is tough and we need to celebrate when we achieve something of significance.

After a victory I think it's important to celebrate and then to refocus so you can go again. Most people use New Year's resolutions as the optimal time and most companies use end of quarter as their time. In tennis after achieving or missing a goal I would sit down and really think about it, refocus, set new goals and off I'd go again.

One of my coaches along the way was Peter Clarke. Peter was an Irish Davis Cup player who grew up in Australia. He came back to Ireland and represented us in Davis Cup. He was in the team the generation before me. He coached me a little bit during the summers when I was home from college. I also travelled with him to one or two events. Peter was a very good player and his highest singles ranking was 229 ATP. He was a great coach and helped me a lot. He wasn't the most technical coach in the world but he was super positive about everything. He is one of the most positive people I've ever met. I remember one day he said to me, "Never get too high or too low after wins and losses." He is absolutely right. You might win a great client and that's wonderful, be happy, acknowledge and celebrate it, but if you lose a client then don't be down in the dumps. As best you can stay along an even keel.

You must break the goal into smaller parts

I believe that focusing on the micro and process will help you achieve that big scary goal you have. It's important to step back from the goal and break it into smaller parts. If you are a salesperson it's getting into the mindset of what are the little things that I can do on a daily basis that can help me achieve my vision. What is the goal? And work backwards from it. In sporting terms I think about being back on the professional tour and knowing exactly what I needed to do in all areas of my life to help me achieve my goal ranking.

It will give you the confidence to achieve

When I was on the tour I was training in the national tennis centre in Dublin. I've always struggled in the gym. I actually think it's been my mindset. I am not the most athletic person in the world and am not blessed with quick feet. There was a time where I would avoid the gym or be embarrassed about it because I just wasn't good at it. I wanted to stay on the court. When I was training in the national centre I wasn't training hard enough. I wasn't excelling in the environment. Then through Facebook I saw an old trainer of mine from my junior days had opened a gym in Dublin. John Connor is the founder of the Irish Strength Institute. I reached out to John and went to the gym to catch up.

As soon as I walked in and met with John I knew it was for me. The gym was private and John is extremely smart and just an all-round good person. He changed my mindset and the approach to the gym and I had a programme with him which was broken down where I knew exactly what I was doing week to week. He helped me gain confidence in the gym and the big thing was I knew it was really benefiting my tennis. I worked with John for the rest of my career and he was a huge part of my tennis and my move up the rankings. The programme was broken down into simple achievable milestones and he was the first trainer that actually got me enjoying the gym.

I'm a huge sports fan and pretty much watch every sport around. I enjoy it all. Rugby is a sport I like watching on TV especially the Ireland games. One of the legends of Ireland rugby and the former captain is a man from

Limerick, Paul O'Connell. He retired a few years ago but he always had that mental fortitude that I loved. I saw him give a keynote on performance recently and I thought he was very good. There was one quote that stood out for me. He said during rugby there is so much going on during a game with players flying in from everywhere. What he realised was that he needed to 'win the moment in front of his face'; he needed to beat the guy in front of him and focus on the small details. If you have a sales call coming up but all your thinking is about your next meeting, how can you deliver on that sales call? Focus on the little things and that will give you confidence then to go and focus on the big things

With my company HC Collective I do a lot of one to one coaching both in person and remotely, team programmes and speaking appearances. However, I didn't just do this one day. The idea stemmed from Necker when I was coaching Richard. He would host groups and events on the island where they might speak about things like climate change or leadership etc. While I was on Necker I sat in on some of these events and very much enjoyed them. I had an epiphany where I thought why can't I do my own events in Dublin?

With events, especially early on, you need something called a lynchpin or a name. Dan Kiely who is the co-founder of Voxpro is a good friend of mine and I asked him if he would attend. He is well known and respected in business and I knew other guests would like to meet him. I started with a 12-person CEO event and the topic was leadership. I have gone on to host bigger and smaller events over the last few years. That small 12-person event gave me the confidence to do bigger and bigger events until I actually realised that I enjoy the smaller events more. By breaking that goal into small details it will give you the confidence to go and achieve it.

It helps you manage the goal

Breaking the goal into smaller parts helps you manage the goal of what you're trying to achieve. It also gives you focus which is an absolute key. You can only manage what's in front of you and it's important to focus on those small details.

When the goal is broken into smaller parts it helps you see what's achievable. I'm always saying to go after your dreams, you only live once etc, but at the same time you need to be realistic. The goal has to be manageable. If I have five kids I'm not going to set a goal to run for four hours a day seven days a week, it's just not manageable. I need to be on top of the goal and it needs to be realistic. When I left college I had been ranked as high as 3 in college doubles and never been ranked in collegiate singles. Someone said to me, "I think you could make the top 100 in singles." I laughed because it was just not credible. You need to be able to manage the goal effectively.

While I was at college at LSU my coach was Jeff Brown. Jeff is a great person. A lot of players go to college in the US and play for an angry drill sergeant who makes them run all day. These players burn out and end up quitting tennis. Jeff wasn't like that. We worked very hard but it was out of respect for him and the programme he had built. He was a calm, easy-going but tough coach. It felt like you could approach him with anything and he was just an all-round good guy. I actually remember very little of college classes but I do remember one thing Jeff used to speak about. He used to say when there is a night out and your friends are begging you to go out and you say no and they keep asking, well everyone has been in that situation: "You have to come out, come on." His message was that their night doesn't end if you don't come out, they will be just fine. I used to think about that and again it's back to managing the goal. If I went out every night I would lose control and not be able to achieve what I set out to.

It gives you clear objectives

Breaking your goals into smaller parts gives you those small clear objectives. With Kevin Clancy my sports psychologist we broke the goal into a results chart that I needed to hit. Every time I hit them I would take my pen out and tick them off and be one step closer. However, can we go further than that and ask the question what you need to do on a daily basis to help you hit that goal? How many serves do you need to hit a week? And how much shoulder rehab do you need to do? In business how many calls do you need to make? Or what are the daily tasks that need to get done?

One thing I have seen in teams in my corporate work is that sometimes there are KPIs there that might be, say, make 20 calls a week. A person ends up making the 20 calls but doesn't care about the quality. When you set goals and have those clear objectives there needs to be a focus put on the quality as much as the quantity. In the book *Outliers* Malcom Gladwell talks about the 10,000-hour rule to master any skill. Simply put, Gladwell explains that reaching the 10,000-hour rule, which he considers the key to success in any field, is simply a matter of practising a specific task that can be accomplished with 20 hours of work a week for 10 years. However, it's not 10,000 hours for the sake of it. It's 10,000 hours of deliberate practice and the word deliberate is very important. It's the quality hours that count.

In the months leading up to the Guinness World Record we were working with Leo and were doing a lot with breathwork. Every Sunday I would look at my diary and see where I could pencil in my breathwork every day. By breaking that goal down into daily short sessions it gave me clear objectives to help me go and break that big goal of being a Guinness World Record holder. At the end of every day I would go and tick off my work completed. It was clear I knew what I had to do and was moving one step closer.

I work with a lot of corporate sales teams that are looking to hit their goals. What I would do typically is survey them anonymously for feedback to understand the temperature of the team. I'd speak to them one to one to hear the issues and design an offsite or day away to discuss the things going well but also the things that need to improve in order to move the team forward. At the end of the session the team leaves with clear objectives which someone in the team owns to ensure they are delivered on. If there is a big problem in the team, it's still broken into small parts and in a clear objective of what the individual can do on a daily basis to get the team back on track.

You need to define your vision

In Chapter 1 we spoke about the importance of defining your vision, but when it comes to your vision there are a couple of key points to make.

You need to be all in

When I went to Necker for the first time in 2015 I met a man who I have so much respect for. He is such a good person and has been a very good supporter of mine over the years. His name is Tim Gannon and he is the founder of Outback Steakhouse which is a famous American restaurant. There are 1,200 Outback restaurants in 23 countries including North and South America, Asia, Europe and Australia. Tim invented what's known as the Bloomin' Onion which is a fried seasoned onion and they sell 15 million Bloomin' Onions a year alone! Tim has an incredible story and I keep encouraging him to write a book. In 2016 he was honoured at an event with the Ireland Funds for an Irishman of the Year award. I got a message a few months before the event asking me if I would be his guest at this event. I flew out to Palm Beach Florida and spent one of the best weeks of my life playing tennis and hanging out with Tim. When you spend time with Tim you realise just how all in he is to achieve his goals. He's started a new fast casual restaurant with his son Chris called Bolay and they already have 15 of them in basically no time at all.

When I spent my first month with Sir Richard Branson on Necker Island in the summer of 2016 I played tennis with him twice a day for the month. Of the 30 days we played tennis on 28 days. He just never stops. I would have a cup of tea with Richard before every tennis session and maybe even during! Richard was also training for the Virgin Strive event in aid of Big Change which connects and supports organisations that can create positive change for young people. I have to be honest that when I heard about the Virgin Strive event or Richard doing a charity fitness event I thought maybe he just shows up at the end to cut a ribbon and take some pictures. That couldn't have been further from the truth. Richard was training like a professional athlete and I have so much respect for what he put his body through to prepare for Strive.

There was one day where he went to Tortola for an insane bike climb. I was told how hard it was going to be and thought no way he's playing tennis this evening. He came back from it and looked exhausted, which he was, and then said, "Give me an hour and I'll be down for some tennis." I remember thinking how is this guy doing this? We played tennis and were sitting having a cup of tea. He was speaking about his body, training and a little on business. I can't remember the exact question I asked but I do remember the exact answer. He said, "Relentless." You have to be relentless. His vision was to finish that Strive event and he was relentless with his training. I learned so many lessons from him and when you look at all his business endeavours he has that relentless streak to go and achieve his vision.

Kurt and Teresa Long are probably the most inspirational business people I've met. They are incredibly successful yet humble and Kurt especially has been a great mentor to me. Kurt worked for Nasa launching rockets and then went on to successfully exit several companies including his last company Fair Warning which is cloud-based security solutions providing data protection and governance for electronic health records, Salesforce, Office 365 and hundreds of other cloud applications. They are such nice people and have both been great mentors to me.

I asked Kurt his advice on my career and the first thing he said to me was, "What's your vision? You need to be clear on that before you can achieve anything." It's a funny one because it's easier said than done. I'm not asking you what your company's vision is but what's your personal vision? When I go into corporates and see these funky offices with missions and values across the wall it looks great. However, a key question which sometimes as an individual we forget is what's our vision? Where are we going? And how are we going to get there?

It's hard to achieve without one

Transition throughout your career is tough. It's difficult if you have been in a corporate job for a significant amount of time and you transition into a new role. It's also difficult in sport. You're trying to reach the top of the mountain and you do, or you don't, then you need to look for a new mountain to climb. From the outside people think when you reach the top of the mountain that you have made it and everything is great, when in reality it's not always the case. Finishing my tennis career it took me a significant amount of time to define my vision. You need to craft it, speak to people, understand yourself and think about what you want to achieve. With all that being said it's hard to achieve without having a clear vision.

I think sport is much easier to define. In tennis you get tested every week too. My ranking was 145 and it's all online around what I achieved and didn't achieve. I always remember meeting people during my tennis days and they would say, "What's next?" I'd come back with, "Well I'm 200 in the rankings and am going to France, Germany and Spain over the next three weeks." It was all so clearly defined. Then I met people after my career and they would ask, "Well what's next?" and I didn't have a clue. I need to define a vision and work through it.

I thought it was just me but as I got into the one to one executive coaching space I started to realise that everyone is trying to figure things out. I have worked one to one with CEOs and senior business people where from the outside it looks like everything is amazing but in reality they are going through their own identity of trying to figure things out. I hosted a mastermind which was an event for 16 business people to come and learn from keynote speakers and learn from each other in an intimate setting. I made the point that throughout my sports and business career I've struggled with imposter syndrome. Never quite confident that I belong in the environment. It's amazing what doubt can come into our minds. The majority of the time it's all in our heads. During the mastermind pretty much every one of the 20 business people attending had suffered from imposter syndrome at one time or another.

You can tell people your vision

It's important to tell people your vision so they can question it and challenge you on it. Don't get me wrong, I'm not saying you have to go and shout it from the rooftop. It very much depends on someone's personality but it's important to talk to people around their vision. My executive coach Stephen Twaddell has very much helped me around that. During my career he has heard me say all sorts of things about what I was going to do next. He has been able to ask me those questions that make me think. Things like, "Is this aligned with your values?" or "What's with the change in behaviour?" I think it's important you have some impartial person to question you around your vision.

I think if you tell people your vision and really believe it then people will support you and get behind your vision. I started hosting my events and telling people at the start what I was going to do before I went to market with my offerings. At the time I didn't have a huge amount of experience but people supported me to bring me in to do little bits of work to get me off and running. I think if you are authentic with people and tell them your vision they will try to help you. Too many times we are afraid to ask. The worst thing someone can do is say no.

When you take that step back and think about your direction and start to get clear on your vision then it would be good to sit down and talk it through with a group of mentors. Dr Betty introduced me to the concept of the internal boardroom about who can you call on for advice. I sat down with a few business friends to discuss my vision and what they thought. They actually looked at it and asked me questions that opened my eyes to the fact that maybe it wasn't the right way to go. If I hadn't told these people my vision I would have got lost down a rabbit hole that would have been difficult to come back from.

CHAPTER 3

LOOKING AT THE FACTS

You need to look at the facts and indicators to understand if you can achieve your vision in the future. No matter how much training I do I'm not going to be able to run the 100 metres in under 10 seconds. I'm just not as the facts don't say so. Facts should be used as an indicator if it's likely for you to achieve your goals. Of course there are outliers but generally it should give you a good guide on what's possible.

You can achieve this goal the facts say so

You need to look at your previous achieved goals. My initial goal graduating from LSU was to break inside 250 in the world. I had been ranked as high as 3 in college and had played and beaten several players that went on to be ranked extremely high. Indications were I could do it. This gave me confidence and the indicators pointed to the fact that this was an achievable goal.

Look at previous achieved goals

After I began facilitating corporate lunches with different topics, one of the CEOs came to me and asked me to facilitate a programme with his team. This had been one of my big goals but I was naturally nervous about it. So I took a step back and thought I've facilitated discussions among these CEOs at my events so there is no reason that I can't do it for a commercial team. I heard a quote from someone that improvement comes on the edge of chaos. We need to put ourselves in uncomfortable positions if we are going to push forward and achieve our goals. I knew I could do this and we all have to start somewhere. I wasn't just purely thrown in, I had done similar things which ensured I had that little bit of confidence and the facts indicated things would be OK, and they were.

When I was under 18 a big goal of mine was to win Irish nationals held at Fitzwilliam Lawn Tennis Club in Dublin. This was our Holy Grail or Irish version of Wimbledon. It was important to me at the time and I wanted to win. James McGee was the number 1 seed and in-form player. He is a better athlete then me and was the favourite to win. In a senior event two weeks before I played against him he beat me 7-6 in the third set. I was disappointed after the match but I distinctly remember my mum asking afterwards if I would prefer to win Lansdowne or Fitzwilliam. Two weeks later I played him in the final and beat him 7-5 in the third set. My previous goals and performances indicated that I wasn't the favourite but I did have a chance to win and believed I could.

I am someone that likes meeting people and giving them advice. I like seeing if there's a way to help them. I was asked by someone if I would coach them on performance on their goals. I was not qualified but had been coached and it was something that was very interesting to me. I looked into courses and started to do my executive coaching qualifications. I enjoyed the course and started my coaching career. I needed to achieve this goal to be comfortable coaching someone.

There is a difference between coaching and mentoring. I can mentor a tennis player and give them my advice whereas in coaching the client has the answer, you are just trying to draw that from them. Early on when I had that element of doubt going in to coach a client I pulled myself back and said wait I've achieved the coaching goal and I'm qualified to do this. Sometimes we lose sight of the facts and the goals we have already achieved.

You are good enough

After I retired from professional tennis my first real job was in recruitment. My role was very much around business development and working with athletes around career transition. I very much enjoyed working with a group of people I liked and for the most part had a good experience. The actual role wasn't what I wanted to do but jobs are stepping stones to get clear on your vision. This job helped me get clear on what I liked and didn't like. I would say it's unusual that your first job is going to be something you want to do for the rest of your life.

Sometimes it's getting clear on what you don't want to do as much as what you do.

I do remember my nervousness around going to meetings and if someone asked me a question I didn't know the answer to. From the outside people would have said I'm relaxed and easy going but on the inside there was a distinct fear of screwing up. I can't remember a moment but I think I grew in confidence and also started to understand the value I was bringing to the business. I took a step back and thought this business isn't a charity. They wouldn't keep me around if I wasn't adding value and I am good enough.

I suffered with a little bit of this in my tennis career too. I remember doing well in Futures which are the lowest end of the professional circuit. When I walked into these tournaments I expected to win or make the final. My ranking had reached a ceiling and I needed to start going to the higher level Challenger events. It was touch and go whether I would get in the draw but I went to Russia for a Challenger event. I remember needing someone to practise with and putting my name down as looking. A top 100 singles player, Karol Beck, signed his name beside mine and I thought oh no this guy will think I'm terrible. We practised and as you guessed everything was fine. He didn't care about me and why should he? But I was good enough and needed to believe in myself. This again is a form of imposter syndrome and it's amazing how many people actually go through it. We always get to see someone's best self but sometimes it's hard to understand or know exactly what people are going through.

Before a Davis Cup tie our captain Gary Cahill arranged a friendly fixture against a team from Sweden. This was a good idea to prepare for our Davis Cup match. One of the guys who travelled with the Swedish team was the retired Magnus Gustafsson. Magnus had been as high as 10 in the world in singles. In his heyday he had one of the biggest forehands in the world. He was actually on my list of favourite players and it was such a pleasure to meet him.

Both teams went for dinner after the friendly match and we asked Magnus for advice. I distinctly remember what he said. Everyone is nervous. You think that the person across from you is not nervous but they are and you recognise that. We even see that with the great Serena Williams as she tries to tie and break Margaret Court's record. Serena is probably the greatest tennis player of all time yet she still gets nervous.

In business and sport we all have these feelings of doubt and are a little unsure of ourselves at times. The lesson I learned through the years was this is OK and the chances are the other person is feeling it too.

Look at your form

You need to look at your previous form as an indicator. I go horse racing once or twice a year. I actually wish I went more but just don't get the time. When you buy the programme and look at the form you can read about the horse and what they have done in previous races. You need to understand that sometimes a long shot wins but generally it's the horses that have shown some kind of form that come out on top.

In 2015 I was coming to the conclusion I would stop playing professional tennis. I needed to take my head out of the bubble and saw the Irish Institute of Sport was hosting an event for high-performance athletes at LinkedIn in Dublin. It was the first time I'd ever gone into a US corporate like this and it was cool. There was a vibrant culture and I thought this place is interesting. Alan Temple who was the manager of a sales team, former amateur rugby player and huge sports fan, gave us a talk on how important LinkedIn was for our careers. I don't even think I knew what LinkedIn was at that time but his team helped us create our profile.

I always make a point of thanking someone afterwards and I went over to Alan to say thanks. Alan is funny, high energy and just good fun. I told him my story and he kindly said he would be happy for me to come on to his team and do a little work experience. I could sit in on sales calls and learn what his team do. For the next few months I did this and loved it. Aisling Jiang who was on his team was a great supporter of mine and couldn't have been more helpful.

After a few months of casually coming in Alan asked me if I would like to do a mock interview which consisted of a mock sales call. I was nervous but did it. In the end I remember thinking I need to look at the facts and specifically look at my form. I loved the place, people and culture and still do. There's no doubt it's a cool place to work, but when I looked at the actual roles it was not something that interested me and I moved on. I took the learnings and moved on.

Tennis wise I needed to look at my form too. In sport it's easy to do this. You are under the microscope every week and you can google me this second and check my results. After making it to 250 my next goal was to make it inside 200 then 150 and then 100. It was gradual steps and I constantly needed to look at my form along the way. I had beaten several top 100 singles and doubles players throughout my career so my form indicated I could do it. If I was unranked and losing every week in the first round to other unranked players then you would say I've lost the plot. Your form should give you some indication that you can achieve your goal.

There are outliers and I do think this is why we love sport and business where things happen that don't make sense. I met the most brilliant entrepreneur at the Necker Cup in 2015 and we have remained friends ever since. Her name is Tonya Lanthier and she started a company called Dental Post from her kitchen in Atlanta. Tonya is a dental hygienist by background and noticed a gap in the market for dentists looking to post jobs. She has scaled the company to help connect and educate 800,000 job seekers in the US and Canada. Sometimes it's hard to understand why in business we succeed or fail when the facts are stacked against us. She had lots to do to make the business work and she has. Her form and how she slowly built the company has led to great success for Dental Post and I'm sure the company will continue to expand.

You must trust yourself

Deep down, you must trust yourself too. The gut is a powerful thing and sometimes we have a feeling what we are doing is right even if it goes against other people's opinion.

When you know you know

I had come to the end of the road tennis wise in 2015. I wasn't playing great on the court but the bottom line was I wasn't enjoying it as much as I used to. I think in business and sport there's a tendency to stay on too long and merely float along when you should just exit stage left. I can't remember the talk I watched or even the person giving the talk but what she said was, "When you know you know."

I lost a match in Italy in a place called Manerbio and after that match I said to myself I'm done. I don't know if it was gut or intuition or what but I had the feeling that the time was right to put my racket away. I went on to play a few tournaments in the US but that was just a holiday and I had made my mind up by that trip. Trust your gut and make that decision that you know needs to be made.

You must trust yourself but you do also need that moment to reflect. I was staying in a hotel on the side of the road in Italy. Let's just say it wasn't glamorous. I was going to eat at this crappy little restaurant beside the garage. Granted it was Italy and the food is incredible so please don't feel sorry for me, but I remember walking back to the room and crying my eyes out. I'm actually not a big crier but this wave of emotion came over me and I couldn't stop. When I eventually did stop crying I had a feeling of well I needed that and it was time to move on. Deep down I had the sense that the time was right.

I ended up working in recruitment for close to two years. I wish I had exercised the same strength in decision making here. I feel I stayed in that job too long and it wasn't for me. I knew a lot sooner than I told them that I wanted to leave. Too many times in life we float along not doing what we want to do and we have to be careful of that. I understand that we have bills to pay and life does get in the way but we owe it to ourselves to find our own path. The recruitment job was something I needed at a time in my career but I needed to move on and I did.

I would encourage you that if there's a burning desire or something you should be doing then go and do it, or if you know your current role isn't working for you then try and change it. I've learned that in sport and business and I'm a strong believer that when you know you know. People like to say the universe will take care of you. I'm not sure I'm a believer of that but, if you protect the downside and you can continue to pay your bills and you will be happier in life, then why not do it?

No one really cares

You will read throughout the book about the many great people and mentors that I've met through my life and career. I've been very fortunate to meet these people and I encourage you to get people in your corner to help drive you forward. That's why in some ways I'm uncomfortable saying that no one really cares about you, but in some ways it's true. Everyone is busy going their own way and living their own life. I noticed this with tennis. Tennis goes on and you might be a conversation piece but you're quickly forgotten. I had friends on the tour that I'm still very much in touch with and I also had friends on the tour that paid you lip service but when it comes down to it they weren't really friends. No one owes you anything.

In my job in recruitment I remember being there a short time and someone significant left the business. It was long since forgotten and people just move on. I'm not sure what I was expecting but it did teach me that you need to look after yourself. It was acknowledged and it wasn't that anything was done wrong but the person is quickly out of sight and out of mind.

When I played college tennis at LSU the same thing happened. You get presented with a picture thanking you for your service but in the background the coaches have been desperately trying to find people to replace you. Obviously there is absolutely nothing wrong with this but I do feel that you need to look after yourself and achieve your own vision and goals.

There are people who care about you and that's your family and close support group. My point is that group is not going be 100 people and it's more likely to be your family plus three or four. I've been lucky in that I know exactly who these people are and can go to them for advice. Find those people who care because no one else will. It can be tough when you lose one of these people from your support network. My girlfriend broke up with me and I found it incredibly hard as I didn't quite understand the reasons. Hopefully someone in your support network will step up and help. In my family my sister Amy was a huge support to keep me going. The same is true in business and we all need people in our corner to talk to.

Your mind is powerful

Your mind is an extremely powerful thing. We have all seen videos around what people can do when they put their mind to it and how if you approach things with a positive mindset then good things will happen.

My first Davis Cup cap came in 2006 against Slovenia at Fitzwilliam Lawn Tennis Club when I was 19 years old. This was a dream come true for me and one of my life goals. I was playing college tennis for LSU at the time and had been doing well in doubles. I came back to Ireland for the summer and played well domestically and was picked for the team. I actually didn't think I would start the match against Slovenia and thought the captain who was Owen Casey at the time would start with more experienced players. I was on cloud 9 at the time and was buzzing for the week.

On the Friday night we were 2-0 down after the singles and the doubles was Saturday afternoon. I remember there was a knock on the door on the Friday evening and it was Owen. He just said, "You're in for doubles, how do you feel?" I was buzzing, absolutely buzzing. The first person

I called, and that never changed throughout my tennis career, was my mum. I always wanted to make my parents proud and still do, and I knew they would be delighted. Again it's those people that we have in our corner. We all know that when we get an exciting piece of news the first thing we want to do is tell our friends and family.

Now to think of the match. We played against Grega Zemlja and Luka Gregorc. I played with Kevin Sorenson. I remember being in the changing rooms before the match looking in the mirror and muttering, "Want the ball." I was getting in the frame of mind to just go for it. At the time you never know if you will get another cap and I just wanted to enjoy it and have no regrets after it. I went out there and wanted the ball. We were the underdogs and were actually winning the match two sets to one but ended up losing 7-6 3-6 6-3 3-6 5-7 in the fifth set.

I was proud of the way I played and have good memories from the match even though we were disappointed to lose. I've played a lot of matches where I've had that mindset but some where I didn't. I believe the same is true in business. In a meeting you have to be confident and have the right mindset. You can't shrink in the corner. I think sport has taught me that lesson.

It's incredible how powerful our mind is and how it's important to get in the right frame of mind. If you're having a one to one meeting, giving a presentation or making a sales call, it's important to show up with the right mindset.

My brother Stephen is probably one of the most inspirational people I've ever met. He is a true example of mindset and making the best of the hand you have been dealt. He is two years older than me and when he was 17 he was involved in a freak farming accident and was paralysed from the neck down. It was a traumatic time for him and our family. Although paralysed he has gone on to live a full life and has done more things than most able-bodied people. He has his own company and is one of the most driven people I've ever met. He has this mindset that is unbreakable and has the ability to just keep going.

The mind is powerful and you need to read relevant facts or pieces of information that give you confidence to go and achieve. If your sales target is £100k and you did £500 k last year then the facts do not indicate that you will be able to hit the £100k. However, I think if you have the right mindset you can excel but need the facts to be realistic on what you can achieve.

You must trust good people around you

A constant theme throughout the book is that you must seek out good people. This is essential. As I said before, sometimes it can feel like no one cares about you, but some people really do.

I had a conversation with Dr Betty Uribe around career development and your journey. It was at a time in my life where I was unsure what direction I was going in. She asked me, "Who is in your internal boardroom?" I had never heard of this before. Her point was that companies have their boardroom. There is a chairman and directors etc. That's for a company, but as an individual who are the people in your corner? I would encourage you to create an internal boardroom. Write down three or four names that will be champions for you and ask them for advice when you need it.

I have hosted several C-suite events for CEOs over the last few years. One of my favourite people in the world is Val Quinn who is the global customer director for Coca-Cola. The question was asked around the table about mentors and should you have one. Her point was not to have one mentor but to have several. She has a mentor in several different areas and people she can approach for advice.

Val's point made me think of one of my favourite authors Robin Sharma who said, "Surround yourself with the people you want to become." When I was playing tennis professionally doing pre-season in December in Ireland was difficult. The facilities were not world class and it was tough with the cold conditions. We have some indoor courts in Ireland but not heated so it means that if it's -1C outside then it's likely to be the same temperature inside.

I was ranked 200 at the time and a very good friend of mine Purav Raja who was ranked 100 asked me to come to India to do pre-season with Mahesh Bhupathi and Rohan Bopanna. They were the number 3 ranked team in the world and Mahesh is considered one of the best players of all time. I went and did a month's training block with them and spent my Christmas eating chicken curry.

It was a sacrifice worth making and my performance levels went up greatly.

I trusted Purav that he was bringing me to a good training camp which was great for my tennis. I learned as much spending time off the court with these guys as I did on the court. It's all about standards and expectations and it's important to put yourself around good people. What I learned was that it's all about standards. The standards were higher at the highest level. The work rate was up a notch. For me training in Ireland I was a big fish in a small pond. I was the best doubles player whereas when I went to India I was the hitting partner who needed to prove himself and was practising with the best in the world. As an individual or business person what can you do to get around the best and learn from them? If you are a small business and want to be a big business, how are you going to do that? You need to learn from the people that have done it.

In 2016 I was on Necker and I was lucky to spend a week with Crystal Sacca of Lowercase Capital. Her husband Chris was one of the sharks on *Shark Tank* and they run Lowercase Capital which was one of the best performing VC funds ever. Crystal likes to play tennis and we have kept in touch ever since our week playing on Necker. Crystal is an amazing person. She told me about her book *The Essential Scratch and Sniff Guide to Becoming a Wine Expert* and I told her I had ambitions to write a book at some stage. She encouraged me and basically said why not? One email she sent last year said 'when's the book coming out?' We all need to seek out good people.

Positive people make a world of difference

It's crucial to seek out people for advice but it's equally crucial to seek out positive people that you trust and will make an impact in your life. Dan and Linda Kiely who are the founders of Voxpro are good friends of mine. They are incredible and unique people. Voxpro was founded in 1999 by Dan and Linda over a pub in Cork. It now has offices in Dublin, Sacramento, San Francisco and Bucharest. The company went on to have 2,349 employees before they exited the company in 2017. They are tennis fans and came to Necker for several Necker Cups. I feel like they make a great team. Dan is a super positive, charismatic, eccentric entrepreneur. He is not a facts and figures man and anything is possible. Linda is much more measured and focused and in some way realistic. They make an excellent team. Positive people on your team will make the world of difference but we also need to have the more measured people who can help deliver. They are an incredible example of a mixed skill set.

One of my takeaways from coaching Sir Richard Branson is just how positive he is. When we would have our tea in the morning there was no topic off the table. I love the news and reading the paper. I do it every day religiously. I remember feeling that Richard would always put a positive spin around most things. As people we need to find a way to put ourselves around positive people.

The right team is crucial

Getting the right team and mix of people is incredibly important for high performance and to achieve your individual or team goals. It's easier said than done but of the utmost importance.

I work with several teams around performance. I worked with a tech team in London that were trying to hit their target. One of the core components to getting the right team is to get accurate feedback. I would send a survey with a list of powerful questions to gather data as to what was going on. Then I would meet with each team member one to one or on a hangout to discuss both their and the team's challenges. When you design a day or two days to bring the team into the room it's amazing to see how people hold things in. It's my job as the facilitator to bring that out of them. It's crucial to have a high-performing team and to have the right team where everyone is honest while being respectful.

In 2007 at LSU we were ranked 12 in the nation. We had a great team. We ended up beating Illinois that year 4-3 and they went on to make the final of the NCAA losing to one of the greatest college teams ever in the University of Georgia. We were unlucky because probably our best player Michael Venus was ineligible to play for us that year so had to sit on the sidelines. If he *had* been eligible I'd be interested to see where we would have ended up.

Indeed, that was the best team I've played in. We were a close team and were all striving and pushing each other along. The standards were high and everyone was working hard. One thing that was hugely beneficial was we did several activities as a team. That year we had 12 players in the team with six being from the US and six being from

Europe. We did several challenges where we played them in touch football, football, golf, bowling and so on. This was great for team camaraderie.

I have found this hugely beneficial when it comes to company offsites. It's important to sit down and look at the facts and data to help move the team forward but another thing that's overlooked and is very important is to get people out of their work environment and spend time socially with their teammates.

If there are people who are not good for the team and bringing the team down, as a team leader and for the good of the person and for your team, you need to move them on as quickly as possible. One CEO I worked with said she would sit down with them, delve into their values and see what's important to them. People are smart and they generally know when something isn't working. She said that by having this deep dive conversation people realise that maybe this specific role isn't for them. Maybe there is a suitable role for them within the organisation or maybe there isn't, but you have to do what's best for everyone involved.

CHAPTER 4

ACHIEVING YOUR GOALS

Sometimes we lose sight of the fact that we have achieved goals both big and small before and we should acknowledge and celebrate that.

It's hard to achieve big goals. I remember when I first broke into the top 200 in doubles I was working with Conor Taylor who is a great coach. You won't meet a nicer person then Conor. He kept telling me how proud I should be of my ranking and how I should celebrate it. I didn't need to go out and get drunk but acknowledge that I'd achieved a big goal.

As an individual or a team we spend a quarter of the year chasing. At the end of the period of time we should go and celebrate this and mark it as it should be. It's not easy to achieve a goal and if you do then celebrate it.

One thing to be acutely aware of is the danger of burnout. This is a challenge in sport or business life. I see it extensively in my work in corporate life. Again we are chasing these big goals whatever they may be. It's crucial that you have time factored in to take stock before you go again. You need to listen to your mind and your body. It's important to check in with your goals to see if they are encroaching on the rest of your life. It's also important to not lose focus of the important people you have in your life. Goals are important but it's important to have a personal life too.

In coaching one of the most used tools is the 'Wheel of Life'. The wheel is simply there to look at all areas of your life and gives a good snapshot on how balanced your life is. Sometimes your career might be a 10 but your personal life is at a 3. Can we bring the wheel more into balance and have your career at an 8 and your personal life at a 7? Try to balance things out. I have fallen victim to this from time to time and been too focused on my goals. I have also had people in my personal life who didn't understand how important a balanced life is.

Goals are not easy to achieve. In fact, if they were easy everyone else would be doing it. However, they are incredibly fulfilling and rewarding if you're going after the correct goals for you. I still laugh when I think back to a comment someone made to me when I was playing professionally. It was from an Irish player who had stopped playing years ago. It was something to the effect of, "I would have been as good as you if I played as much as you." I thought of the quote 'the harder I work the luckier I get'. That tennis player had ambition but the simple truth is he didn't put the time in. In corporate life it's going to be hard to excel if you don't put a significant amount of time into it.

Include underperformers

In the previous chapter I spoke about moving people on who weren't good for the team. However, there are going to be people or individuals who are underperforming but who are good for the team and can be developed to be high performers.

Maybe you missed your goal the previous month but were close and almost did it. Keep believing in yourself. In college I remember going on this terrible losing streak where I just had no confidence. I think that's the time for the coach to work with you, build you up and give you the confidence to succeed. I found that the coach would naturally gravitate towards the players winning and work with them.

There are two things here. As an underperformer I need to go to my coach or team leader and ask for a meeting and seek help to get me up to speed. There is no point in me just hiding away in the corner and burying my head. As an individual you need to take ownership and be accountable to yourself. If you need help you have to be OK in going out and asking for that help. On the other hand, I think a team leader or coach needs to approach the underperformer, show they care and help bring them back up to speed.

In a team at any one time there is always going to be someone not firing. The stats around mental health are frightening. According to UK stats, 1 in 6.8 people (14.7%) experience mental health problems in the workplace. We just don't know what people are going through in their lives. It's extremely important that when you are in a team you support each other.

When we did the Guinness World Record there was a period of time where Dan O'Neill was struggling in a big way. If you play tennis for 60 straight hours you are going to have your ups and downs. At that time when someone is struggling you need to be there for them, encourage them and be in their corner. We were very lucky that our trainer Leo left his house at 4am to come and support Dan. There are peaks and troughs and we got through this tough time during the night on the court. The sun did come up and Dan did get better. If we had been negative with Dan and told him he was letting us down or left him alone, I don't think we would have made it.

It's important for you to seek feedback as an individual or in a team from a manager. As an individual, approach your mentor or coach for feedback and be open to receiving it. Too many times people say they want to or are open to receiving feedback, but when it comes down to it they have no interest in hearing it.

I worked with a company where the owner said to the group, "I love feedback so please give me feedback." However, when it actually came down to it and you gave this person feedback it was in one ear and out the other.

Even more so than this it was obvious that this person was not even listening to the feedback given.

Recognise contributors

People want to feel valued, appreciated and recognised for the work they have put in. It's important to recognise people for a job well done in a team. As an individual it's important to recognise the people that have supported you.

It's standard in companies to have employee of the month or salesperson of the month etc, but it's important to note that not everyone actually wants to be recognised in such a public way. Some people appreciate a quiet word. One manager of a team I have worked with noticed this. She has incredible EQ and noticed that one or two people would be embarrassed to be called out in front of everyone. She would bring them into a one to one meeting and thank them for everything they had done.

There is incredible power in a handwritten thank you card. It stands out and it's something different. The instinct is to send an email saying thanks. Now that is fine too but there is something to be said for writing a thank you note. People really appreciate how you went out of your way to thank them. I know Richard Branson has written publicly on his LinkedIn blog about the power of a handwritten thank you note.

It's important to make people feel valued. As I work with teams it's amazing what individuals will tell you about what annoys them about other people in the team. One thing that has come up several times in individual chats is when people in meetings have their mobiles on the table. We have all been there sitting across from someone and their mobile is on the table and the light flashes and they look at it. What do you think you are saying to someone on your team? Or in a business meeting? You are not that important to me.

I met a C-suite executive who travels the world and likes to see himself as some kind of high roller. I met him in Dublin and he had two mobiles on the table and checked them every five minutes during our meeting. I understand how this is a little extreme, but I couldn't believe the lack of respect and I walked away thinking I will never do business with this person.

Some companies don't recognise high performers and this is wrong too. It needs to be acknowledged in public or private depending on what the individual wants. I sat down one to one to work with individuals from a tech company and one thing a few of the employees said really struck a chord with me. It was something to the effect of 'If we hit our target or don't then nothing really changes'.

This was shocking to me and should be a complete red flag. If the team hits their target it should be celebrated and acknowledged. Individual high-performing contributors should be recognised and underperformers should be supported. If the team fails to hit the target then a deep dive should be done to understand why and what they can improve going forward.

Your learning from your previous attempts

Goals are hard but it's important to learn from your efforts to understand what you can change or improve going forward. Albert Einstein once said, "The definition of insanity is doing the same thing over and over again and expecting different results."

You must debrief

Whether you succeeded or failed on your goal you need to sit down and debrief and ask the difficult question of why or why not. You have to keep learning. There are too many times in our business or personal life where we chase a goal and then just move on to the next goal. The debrief is crucial. I worked with a high-performing corporate team in London and the company hit their target comfortably, but the manager felt like there was something missing. She was proud and happy the team succeeded but felt they could do even better. From feedback with the team generally everything was going well. When we did the day offsite the team concluded there were some issues around communication that needed to be addressed. We addressed these and the team is excelling. A lot of the time it's very small changes that need to be made to keep pushing the team forward.

In professional sports we see how everything is analysed and looked at constantly. Even the evolution in individual sports like tennis has been incredible. When you look back to 25 years ago a top player would go to a tournament with his/her coach. Now it's a team including a physio, nutritionist, practice partner etc. It's not uncommon to hear an interview where a top player is asked a question and they say, "Well I'll discuss this with my team." As an individual or group we all need a team and it is essential to debrief.

By debriefing you learn lessons. In 2014 we played Davis Cup against Luxembourg. Gary Cahill was the captain and it was his first time captaining the team. Gary is a good coach and captain. This was an interesting tie as there was added interest in it. Great Britain were in our zone for Davis Cup and if we won our match against Luxembourg then we would have played GB and Andy Murray would have played. Tennis in Ireland is a small sport so this would have been huge for its profile. There was a buzz about this tie. However, I remember during that tie feeling a lot of pressure and not really enjoying the tie too much, particularly the preparation. A lot of that pressure was my own shortcomings as a player and some of it was more around the environment.

We lost the tie and afterwards we were asked to give feedback to our sports psychologist. I gave my feedback honestly of what I was feeling. To give Gary credit he was a different captain from then on. He did the debrief, looked at the information, learned from it and moved forward. That is why a debrief can be so powerful but only if you use the learnings and move forward with them. I enjoyed all the ties after that one.

You must stop chasing goals

It seems like a little bit of a contradiction. On one hand you need to be relentless when it comes to going after your goals, but on the other hand don't chase them and listen to yourself.

Sometimes in tennis I lost sight of this and I chased too much. I wanted to move up the rankings and my thought process was I wasn't going to be able to do this sitting at home. One example of this was when I played a Davis Cup match against Egypt in 2014. We won the match but instead of staying with the team and celebrating I travelled to Turkey the next day to play a tournament.

In hindsight I should have celebrated with the team, regrouped and gone to the next tournament. I saw the points in Turkey and I went to play. I ended up losing in the first round. It was a poor decision on my part. As an individual take your time and regroup. Don't rush one goal into the next. You need to look after yourself. The best way to ensure you can achieve a goal is to be fresh and have a clear mind.

In tennis you need to trust your training and the process and it's no different in business. We are all going to make mistakes and it just depends how much you stick to the process. I worked with a well-known tech company and I spent two days listening in on calls they were making to prospective customers. It was incredible to me the process that these people had in front of them. It was literally a script that they didn't often deviate from.

You need to take a deep breath from time to time. In tennis this can be in the heat of the battle. If you lose a long or tough point in tennis you have 25 seconds to regroup, breathe and gather your thoughts. In business if you make a call that doesn't go well, give yourself 25 seconds to breathe, regroup and go again. Sometimes we need to just slow down and take our time even if that's just for a few seconds.

The truth is that you need to challenge each other

In a team there needs to be a challenge there and you need to challenge each other. It is essential that the team has an honest group discussion. This discussion needs to be respectful but to the point. People need to leave a meeting with clarity on how to move forward. One team I worked with had people from all over the world. It was apparent there was tension in the room. As you get people to open up then that one team feeling becomes evident.

In a team environment it's important to have an accurate reading of the team to fully understand the team morale and the issues you are facing. Feedback is a powerful tool but it's important to get accurate feedback so the team can be driven forward. I think we have all been in meetings or situations where we want to say something, know we should say it but don't. We have to think of the best way to get this information from someone. It's key to a high-performing team.

As a team leader in sport, business or as an entrepreneur with an external team, we need to ask tough questions.

It's all about standards and driving those standards. When I went to India for that pre-season training camp with Mahesh Bhupathi and Rohan Bopanna they were ranked 3 in the world. One of the big things I learned was not tennis technique or tactics, it was standards and how you have to have high standards to be a high performer. Forget about what you learn on court, you learn a lot off court with the best in the world. The way they hold themselves and that underlying confidence they have. I think a way to learn is to get around good people.

Purav Raja who was also in the camp works hard but can be lazy. I remember early in the camp he didn't run for a ball and Mahesh stopped and said forcefully, "If you don't start moving your ass then you can leave and don't come back." He meant it too. I thought about myself and if I was in Dublin playing with an Irish kid and he didn't run for the ball. I would have been polite and not said anything. This was a lesson for me in standards. What are your standards as an individual? And as a team?

The same mentality applies

Your mentality needs to be the same as with the previous goals you have achieved. If you have failed on certain goals which everyone has then what lessons have you learned from this to take forward with you?

While on the tennis tour I played doubles occasionally and became good friends with Danish tennis player Fred Nielsen. Fred is a good friend and was a great supporter of mine through the years. He is a philosophical man and honestly one of the most interesting people I have ever met. He is one of the most popular people on tour and very approachable. He was a good singles player with a career high singles ranking of 190 in 2011 and he is also an incredible doubles player with a career high doubles ranking of 17 in 2013.

Fred had never won a tour level match in singles or doubles up until 2012. In 2012 he played the grass court swing of tournaments with British doubles player Jonathan Marray. They did OK playing in the tournaments the level below the highest level. They were lucky to be awarded a wild card for Wimbledon to enter the doubles draw. A wild card essentially means that your ranking is not high enough to gain entry directly but the tournament has a certain number of spots in the draw to award.

These spots in the draw are typically given to home grown players or former champions whose rankings have maybe dropped for whatever reason. Johnny is British and Fred's grandfather Kurt had made the final of Wimbledon in 1953 and they were granted a wild card. They went on to win the Gentleman's Doubles that year and to be honest it's one of the biggest shocks in sport. I couldn't have been happier for Fred and I'm waiting for the Hollywood movie to come out.

I remember having a deep discussion with Fred during a tournament. He mentioned he had worked with a sports psychologist and the guy asked him, "What's your mission?" The point was that every company you go into has this mission statement plastered across the wall or on their website, but as an individual what's your mission? What are you trying to achieve? It's not a goal but almost a higher purpose.

Freddie talked about writing a mission statement for his tennis around the way he wanted to play the game and who he was. He said that at the end of his matches he would read his mission statement to see if he stayed true to the way he wanted to play the game. As an individual I would ask you the question: what's your mission?

It's important that your goals are aligned to the ones you had before. You can achieve your goals because you did it before. If I have pushed my ranking to 500 my next goal is not going to be number 1. It needs to be realistic. I remember a corporate company I did some work with. The company had done fine but failed to hit their target. When we sat down to look at goals for the following year the number they had looked to hit was off somewhere in space.

You have to be ambitious but you also have to be realistic. The team would not believe in the goal they were given and thus would not be that motivated to succeed on it or back themselves to do it. I encouraged the company to rein the goal in and take what they did in the previous year into consideration.

One thing that's important before setting out to achieve your next goal is the recharge. In tennis the off season was so important. A lot of the time you don't want to see a tennis court because of how tired you are from the season. It's important to listen to your mind and body and recharge when you can. It's all relative to your life and what kind of break you can make. In recent years we've seen how big the retreat holiday or wellness break has become. It's whatever works for you and where you are in your life. People with lots of kids don't have the luxury but it's important to recharge. I know my brother-in-law Ed purposely wakes up well before the kids to meditate so he can have some 'me time'. What works for you? But please recharge yourself and go again.

I remember coming home from college one summer and being completely burnt out from tennis. It was a feeling like no other. I had never felt this burnt out or tired of the sport. I remember speaking to my old coach Larry Jurovich and saying, "Larry, I'm going to take two months off and not play tennis, I just can't do it anymore." I remember him saying, "James, don't put any time limit on it, it could be one week, it could be two months or maybe you never want to play again."

Larry knew I would play again but he was right in that I didn't need to put a timeframe on it. The funny thing was I remember I went out a few nights in a row for drinks which is unlike me. I remember then my dad coming into my room at 1pm on day four saying, "What are you doing?" I said, "I'm taking a break," and he said, "Well that's great, you can come and work for me and sweep up over at the office block."

My dad is a retired farmer and owns some property. He doesn't just own it, he's one of those farmers that can and will do everything, whether it's plumbing, electrics or whatever. He is an incredibly hard worker and I think has instilled that in me. On day four I was sweeping at the office block for a while and day five I was back on the tennis court!

I understand in corporate life how it's impossible to take an unlimited break, but it's important to find the time to recharge as you will face burnout and that's never good for the employer or employee. However, there has been a market shift in terms of holidays. I know Virgin for example has brought in unlimited holidays to their business, which is great for employees. The big thing is that people are human and we need to treat them that way. We never know what's going on in someone's life and we need to be conscious of that. A recharge can be a weekend away reading a book or even staying at home. It's merely time to take stock and recharge in order to go again.

Culture is everything

The truth is that culture is everything. It doesn't matter whether it's sport or business, you need to have a strong high-performing culture. As a former professional tennis player it was crucial that I surrounded myself with good people and in the corporate world it's important that you hire good people. When someone has gone through the process and been hired on to the team it's essential the expectations are made crystal clear from both sides. Companies have their onboarding process around deliverables but it's crucial that the expectations are set on what the individual should be contributing to the team.

We have all been in teams where there are negative people. I would be polite about these people and simply say they are not in the right role. They need to be moved on out of the company or moved into a role that is right for them. It happens in sport and business. I remember at LSU when a player joined the team and if they weren't performing then the coaches worked with them to help them improve, but if they just weren't good enough then they didn't last in our team.

One element of creating a high-performance culture is through healthy competition. This can vary on the roles and it's important to understand the philosophies and what motivates certain people, but healthy competition is crucial to performance. When I was 16 I was training in a club with a great group of players. Now tennis is an individual sport but our coach Larry used to always preach the fact that it's usually a few good players that come through and not just one, and we need to push each other.

When I was 16 James McGee who was my tennis rival and friend was winning all around him. He was going to international tournaments and doing very well and was a really great player. He invited me to his club to practise one day. He beat me 6-2 6-1 in no time at all. I remember thinking after this practice that this could go one of two ways. I decided to work hard because I wanted to be able to compete with him, and I did. Create that healthy competition. James helped me improve as a player and we pushed each other. There are exceptions, but as people for the most part we make each other better if the right environment has been created.

There need to be occasions where you focus on developing culture and building team morale. We live in an interesting time where some team members work remotely and rarely have that face to face interaction. I'm all in favour of remote working but there's something to be said about getting a team in a room to build relationships. The ironic thing is that forgetting about the strategy talk and the serious stuff, where you are actively trying hard to improve team performance, a natural level of improvement comes from getting everyone in the same room.

CHAPTER 5

DEVELOPING CONFIDENCE

I actually don't see myself as a details person, I'm more of a vision kind of person. However, I do believe in the power of the detail and it giving you the confidence to go and achieve anything. It's one small step at a time that will help you achieve your vision.

You can get there if you take small steps

Those small steps will help you be successful. If you're training to run a marathon, on day one you're probably not going to run 26 miles. You are going to start small, create a plan and have the long-term vision to go and achieve. One CEO was speaking to me about a friend who was opening a coffee shop. He said that this person spoke about opening 10 coffee shops. His point was to focus on opening one, get it working well and then look to open the second and so on. Executing on the small details will give you the confidence to go and achieve the big goal.

Take yourself out of the plan sometimes

Small steps are essential to achieving your goals. Our plan is important to help us get there. I think it's important to surround yourself with people that have either achieved what you are looking to do or have done something similar. I did two training camps in India with some of the best players in the world and there's no doubt I learned as much at the dinner table as I did on the tennis court. One player who was in the camp was the former world doubles number 1 Sania Mirza. Sania is a superstar in India and a great player. She has won six grand slam titles. One of the things that impressed me most about spending time with her was her attention to detail. She did the small things right on a daily basis. She is a huge celebrity in India yet every day she showed up for practice in the right way. She did her stretching, fitness work and always wanted one more drill or feed.

Taking yourself away from your plan and coming up for air is crucial for success. We are all in a rush and busy being busy. One of my regrets from tennis is that I didn't come up for air more. I was playing tournament after tournament because I wanted to hit my points total to move my ranking up. One of my regrets is not going to bigger tournaments as a practice partner to learn from the best players. This is something I still think about. I was more concerned with achieving points. My philosophy at the time was I have to earn my right to be there with those players. I should have absolutely focused on hitting my goals, but as part of that process committed to every few months going to a bigger tournament to practise and learn from the best players. You learn about the details and those small steps when you see the best people in action.

If you are currently in a team and looking to hit a target and are incredibly busy then it's still incredibly important to reach out to someone in your team or in another team that is the best of the best and go for lunch with them or pick their brains on what makes them successful.

The majority of people have to take small steps

It is incredibly difficult to go from 0-100 when trying to achieve a goal but that is what most people do. The best example of this is our New Year's resolutions. I'm going to go to the gym five days a week, or do x and y. What tends to happen? There is no sustainability around it.

When Dr Betty Uribe asked me to speak to her team at California Bank she knew it was my first real speaking gig. She encouraged me and interviewed me on stage. She didn't come to me and say, 'Oh James, you have never given a keynote before but could you give a three-hour presentation to my team tomorrow?'. I needed to take small steps in order to be able to do something like that. I'm all for throwing yourself in to do something but you do need to be set up for success.

Tennis is a good example of this. The vast majority of players chip away at their ranking year after year improving that little bit. At the end of my first year on tour I was 370 in doubles, year 2 I was 250, year 3 I was 150. I stagnated at times but little by little was chipping away at my ranking. Then there are the exceptions: some young kid comes out and just wins everything. We all wish we were that person in business and life but the majority of time it doesn't happen like that.

I think we think of this when we look at entrepreneurs. The media sometimes bills these people as overnight successes. Sometimes we forget the hard work that these people put in to make their business a success. These people go after their goals and the majority of times it takes time to be an overnight success. Elon Musk who is the founder of Tesla said, "When something is important enough you do it even if the odds aren't in your favour."

People can help you

In terms of taking those small steps and keeping on track with your plan, people can help you. I'm very lucky to have the best parents in the world, especially my mum, which I don't think my dad will mind me saying. My mum is the most supportive, kindest, most brilliant person in the world. She is my biggest fan and encouraged me all the way along with my tennis to go and achieve. She would ask me questions about my ranking and performances and whenever I lost or was on a tough run she was the first person to message me and say 'keep going and things will get better'.

We need people like that in our life especially if you're not a detail focused person and can easily get distracted. My junior coach Larry Jurovich had the biggest impact on my tennis career and life. He was very good to me after my brother's spinal injury accident and I am forever grateful to him. He kept me accountable on my goals and was the one who really preached the detail.

He broke everything down and raised the expectations. I remember him speaking about our training and saying with the intensity of the Irish school system we weren't training enough and needed to push each other more. Historically a coach might say you need to hit x amount of serves per week. Larry would say you need to hit x amount of serves and track your percentages and if you're making those serves. He went much more into the details. It's exactly what the Mathew Syed book *Bounce* says, that you need 10,000 hours to master something but it has to be 10,000 hours of deliberate good practice. Larry got us thinking with that mindset.

My executive coach Stephen Twaddell has been great for me on this front in a business sense. He has been in my corner since I've been in the corporate world and has been nothing but encouraging. I would panic and say to Stephen I don't have enough of x and y and am not doing good enough. He will highlight what I'm doing well and how things take time and I'm doing great, and to focus on the details and on what I can control. You need people like that in your corner.

Be sure to thank these people for being in your corner. I think sometimes we forget to recognise these people and actually say thanks, you have really helped me. This is true in both business and our personal life and I have failed on this at times. People use gratitude journals which are great.

I'm not endorsing that but just be nice and value these people in your corner.

For me one of my key learnings with Sir Richard is he really understands people. I remember he asked me one day about the type of racket he should use. I said I didn't know but a friend of mine owned a great tennis shop in Dublin. Will sent rackets over from Martyn Evens Sports and Richard used one of the rackets and loved it. He asked me twice to send him Will's email. I then got an email two days later from Will thinking it was his friend playing a prank on him. The email read 'Dear Will, thank you for sending over the rackets, going forward you will be my racket consultant. All the best, Richard'. Appreciate when someone does something to help you.

A plan makes things achievable

A plan with specific details helps things become more achievable and attainable. Those details will give us the confidence to go and achieve that goal or whatever the objective might be.

It helps you believe

I mentioned the sports psychologist and business coach Kevin Clancy earlier in the book and how much he challenged and helped me. If I'm honest, before that I would have said yeh my goal is to be this ranking but I have just played every week with no overall strategy. This plan that we devised helped me believe I could do it. I have the exact same mindset for business and I know that I need a certain number of speaking gigs, team development programmes and one to one clients. Things take time but with a detailed plan I have the confidence to go and achieve it.

In preparation for the Guinness World Record, Dave Mullins devised the plan of when we would take breaks. What we decided to do was to get everyone in the room including Leo our trainer to discuss when is the ideal time to take our break, when and what we should be eating and how things would look overall. We had input from everyone and actually when we looked at the plan we designed it looked incredibly achievable. It certainly gave me the confidence to go and achieve.

It helps others believe

It's important to create clarity around what you are chasing. I have mentioned I do a lot of offsites for companies. One of the things that gets talked about is the vision or the targets. It's important to get input from everyone but it's also important to be honest with people about the direction in which things are going. Creating clarity around what you are looking to achieve will help others believe in the plan.

In doubles tennis sometimes you play with different partners. I might arrive to a tournament on the Sunday and sign in to play with a specific partner and play with them on the Monday and actually not know them well at all. A lot of the time when you play with someone in that way the plan is essentially made in the moment. Typically these teams are never quite as effective. When I played with doubles partners for a few weeks or longer we would always sit down and discuss a match plan for how we were going to win this match. I need to instil confidence in my partner and he needs to do the same for me.

To help reinforce the plan and give you and others confidence it's important to share your plan with an accountability partner. You will be enthusiastic from them and really feed off their belief in the plan. When I was on the tour I had several mentors I would bounce my achievable plan off to get encouragement from and I do the exact same in business now.

It's OK for the plan to readjust

Sometimes the plan needs to readjust and that's fine. The key is that you have to be OK with that. Things will go wrong, they are bound to. When I set out to make 250 in the world in doubles a lot went wrong. I got sick one week or injured for three and so on. However, my vision was always on this ranking and I had to be OK readjusting to get there.

One person I worked with in a tech company had set her target for x and was determined to achieve it. However, two weeks in things were not going well and she needed to sit down and readjust the plan and go again. This shouldn't be an issue and stress shouldn't build up until everything potentially falls apart at the end of the month. Never be afraid to regroup and readjust the plan so you can go again. In business one of the buzz words is being agile and you absolutely need to be agile and ready to adapt when you need to.

The plan needs to readjust and you need to be realistic. I have thought about this a lot lately. When I was a kid I would play against the practice wall and imagine that I had just won Wimbledon. I don't think I ever lost against the wall and loved using my imagination. When you get a little bit older you start to realise that winning Wimbledon might be harder and your goals are reined in. My life goal plan is constantly updating.

When you start on the tour your goal is to get an ATP ranking – that's a huge focus and was for me. I remember early on someone would point at a player and say, "Is he good, does he have a point?" To some players getting that elusive ATP point is everything whereas others don't even consider it. You need to be ambitious but you also need to be realistic when it comes to your plan and open to readjusting.

The plan can change and readjust, but a good way to make those changes is based on the data you have received. It's amazing in sport where things have gone since the introduction of data and the information managers and players get. Things are down to a science and it's no different in business. Once you have the data your chances of making a more effective decision go up, but I do say it with a word of caution. I also believe in the power of your gut when making a decision with the aid of good information. I have noticed in corporate life that sometimes we need to go through too many people to make a decision. I think of Richard Branson when he started Virgin Atlantic. He said that if he had spoken to accountants they would have told him he was crazy but he knew he was right. Trust your gut with the help of data.

I have been learning more about conditions including anxiety lately and how that can affect someone's decision making. It can lead to paralysis and also to irrational decision making. It's important to have someone you can talk through these issues with whether that's in your personal life, business or with a counsellor. All you can ever do is look at the facts you have and make a decision which you feel is right.

The details can change but the dream doesn't have to

Sometimes our big vision can stay the same but we learn from the original plan that what we thought to be the best way actually wasn't and we need to readjust. That's OK and we should be comfortable with that. That's where mentors and executive coaches can help. Having someone from outside the bubble to ask you those difficult or alternative questions that poke your vision and help you see if there is a clearer way to achieving it.

You have to be relentless

I mentioned in Chapter 2 about Richard Branson being relentless when it came to achieving his goals. He has an incredible focus about him when it comes to achieving. He is also eager to learn. He never strikes me as necessarily a details type of person. When I coach him tennis I don't give a huge amount of technical detail, it's more around the bigger picture stuff. However, I do give little bits of detail and you can tell that he focuses because he knows it might make his stroke better.

Earlier I mentioned Kurt and Teresa Long. They have had several successful exits and you can't leave a conversation without being inspired by Kurt's sheer knowledge and presence. As a couple they make an incredible team. When you spend time with them you can tell they are relentless when it comes to their business but do it in an empathetic way to their people. Kurt has been a great mentor to me and I have asked him several times about goals. His answer is always, "What's the vision?" You have to have that clear vision. I think once the vision is there you can pivot and change direction and stay on track to achieve it.

You are good enough

Sometimes goals come down to sheer belief and believing you can achieve. I lost several Davis Cup matches for Ireland where I didn't play my best tennis. I probably wasn't the favourite in a lot of these matches but sometimes I think I could have performed better. I remember before our match against Egypt being a little bit nervous; however, I do remember looking in the mirror and speaking to myself saying you are good enough to win and go and enjoy it. We had a great game plan and we did indeed get the win.

Other matches where I lost we also had a great game plan but when it came down to it I simply didn't believe I was good enough to win. It's almost like you need to fake it until you make it. It's easier said than done to believe in yourself but you need to get to that spot and accept we are all human and we all have doubts. Nothing is going to be 100% perfect.

When I was moving up the tennis rankings I was constantly readjusting what I needed to do and the points I needed to make. I would sit down every couple of weeks and see if I was on track. If I wasn't and needed to readjust the goal then I would. In business if you are failing to hit your target, use the power of self-talk and tell yourself you are good enough to do this. You do have to take your learnings and readjust, but you are good enough.

One thing I have noticed about Richard Branson is just how positive he is. Every time I speak to him and ask, "Richard, how's your tennis?" his answer is always, "Better than ever." He's got this positive can-do attitude. Nothing is impossible. I know it's easy to say when you're a billionaire living on a private island, but I think if you're not positive then it's a spiral. You probably will tell yourself you're not good enough and miss your goal. Somehow you have to find the positive in situations.

You need to be agile

Things are naturally going to go wrong but you have to expect that and move forward. The vision can be the same but the details can change on the spot. In tennis it happens all the time. You would go out to play a match with a specific game plan and something happens during the match and you spot something and need to change tactics. There can also be external factors completely out of your control. In tennis it could be the wind. You might need to change tactics based on that.

In the companies I have worked with I see the same thing. Things will naturally go wrong and you have to readjust accordingly. One of the big things around being agile is your mindset. If you enter with the mindset that if something happens you won't be overawed, that's the best approach. I do think a business leader has the ability to help foster this mindset for their team. They need to be positive and understanding of their people. There are some industries where things are too important or it's a matter of life and death if someone makes a mistake. However, in the vast majority of jobs it's not and as business leaders we should be OK with people making mistakes. This is how we learn, grow and move forward.

In the Guinness World Record we had our scheduled breaks to take. We had devised a great plan led by Dave and everyone was feeling comfortable with it. What happened next? On the second night Mother Nature called and I badly needed the toilet so we had to take a break. Another time one of the other players, Dan, was struggling physically and we had to take a break which wasn't in the plan. Now we could have been thrown off by this but we weren't. The vision stayed the same but the details needed to change. The timings and certain aspects needed to change on the spot but we got through it. If we hadn't made a quick decision there as a team then we wouldn't have made it.

I often think of the conference events business where plans change all the time. I have done some group work with an events business and I'm blown away by how much can go wrong in these events. Between speakers pulling out and attendees not happy with something it seems like things happen left and right. It's got to be the ability to be OK with that and take the attitude of 'we are where we are and let's move forward'.

CHAPTER 6

BUILDING YOUR SUPPORT NETWORK

You will notice this theme running through the book around having that support network. I think it's essential to get around successful people with good values. I would encourage you to seek out these people because they are in your network but you need to go out and find them.

There's no doubt in my mind that it's easier with the support of other people. One of the most important things is that they will hold you accountable to what you said you would do. I also think it's good but not always essential that this person is not a spouse or someone too close to you. That's why a coach can be great because they will hold you accountable to your vision and the direction you are going in. It's good to have someone who is impartial that is not afraid to ask you the tough questions. Sometimes I think there's an element that someone very close to you won't tell you the truth when you also need that bit of realism.

Coaching can be expensive if your company is not sponsoring you. My mindset with building a network of people is what value can I add to them. When I approached Stephen Twaddell to coach me I knew he loved tennis so I was able to say, "I'll coach you tennis for an hour and then you can coach me business." It's a reciprocal relationship and we are both giving value.

Leverage other people's experience

It's tough to do it alone and there are a lot of people with experience which you can tap into. While I was on Necker with Chris and Crystal Sacca from Lowercase Capital I was fascinated by how kind they were but also how smart they both are and how successful their fund was. I started looking up interviews with them. One thing which Chris said was that early in his career in Google he would approach the most senior person and ask if he could join their meeting. He was so eager to learn. His value add was he said he would take notes in the meeting. Who is the person or people in your network that you could reach out to and leverage their experience?

Kurt Long, founder of Fair Warning, has been an incredible supporter of mine. Typically we would have a call every month or two and I would ask his advice around what I'm doing and if he sees anything I'm missing. There is a mentor or coach out there for everyone but some people need to get better at asking for that support. Kurt is one of the most successful people I've ever met and is a very busy person, but even if I have a personal problem I know that he will do his absolute best to support me.

I believe that people are inherently kind and they like to help. I hosted a mastermind for business people and I needed one or two speakers. I reached out to Val Quinn who is the global customer director of Coca-Cola and she said yes straight away. I believe in people and their willingness to help when they can. I also believe that relationships should be reciprocal and I have also helped her with one or two things. People can't always help but I do think people are inherently good and they will help if they can.

When I retired from tennis in December 2015 I didn't really know what direction I was going in. I started reaching out to people for help and advice. I went from not really knowing what LinkedIn was to being incredibly active on it and messaging people. I quickly realised how I might be low on business experience but I was OK at hitting a tennis ball around and people like tennis. Tennis is also one to one so you get an opportunity to speak to people and develop a relationship.

The first time I went to Necker in 2015 I met Paul Salem who is well known in the private equity world. I asked him his advice about what I should do and what he said has stayed with me. He said, "Use your tennis to meet great business people and learn from them." His point was that I did well as a tennis player and that's my value add. I believe we can all bring value in different ways and it's to figure out what's your value add.

I reached out and asked people to go for a coffee or a game of tennis. People are busy and I'm not going to say everyone got back to me all the time, but you would be surprised by how many people did. People like to help and support when they can.

One person who has been great to me is Peter Silvester. Peter is a lawyer by background and one of the most connected and nicest men in Ireland. He is a huge sports fan and has a special love for rugby and tennis. I actually think my mind works in a similar way to Peter's in terms of connecting people. When he meets someone he's thinking about who he can introduce that person to. Peter always keeps me in mind for things and from time to time takes tables at events. I sometimes get the call up which I'm inherently grateful for. My point is that you need people like this in your corner as it makes things a lot easier. We need to seek out these good people.

There are also users out there and you need to get better at detecting that, and I do think that comes with experience. I have been burned by people before and I think my radar for people who are users is getting stronger by the day. There's an element sometimes where you are made to feel like a chess piece on a board and you are being used to be moved along. However, my positive experiences outweigh my negative ones and I continue to lead with authenticity and think you should do the same.

Leverage other people's network

We all have our own network of people but then we have to understand that our network has their own network. There is an opportunity to leverage this in a positive way.

One of the keys when you are asking people for a coffee or advice is to be clear on what you are asking. The ask can be as in when I was retiring from tennis that I would like some advice on what I'm doing with my career. There doesn't need to be a huge ask but there does need to be something. I have been asked by people to go for a coffee but when you actually review it there was no outcome. They didn't ask. Just to be crystal clear, the first time you meet someone there's probably not going to be a big ask because you need to build up to that, but the meeting should have a clear outcome.

The big thing which I mentioned earlier but rings true throughout is believe you can add value. With the Chris Sacca Google note-taking example he was absolutely adding value. They maybe wouldn't have been able to capture as detailed notes if he wasn't there. You need to be confident about the value you can bring and bring it. I have been lucky to hang out with a lot of successful people from different types of industries and you see that people are people and no matter who they are we shouldn't be overawed by them.

When I first went to Necker in 2015 and basically had no money, which is what a 150 tennis doubles ranking will do to you, I ended up going back to coach Richard and we became friends. I know that I'm adding value for him on the tennis court and making him better and he's adding value to me with all the great advice he gives me.

I mentioned earlier John Connor who was my fitness coach. John looked after me gym wise and was brilliant. He is the best fitness coach I ever worked with. I added value for John as I sourced one or two clients for him who are still using his gym today. Be confident and think how you can add value. I think when people sometimes go to conferences or networking events their philosophy is what can I get? Or what can I take? Be authentic and try to help people and they will help you.

You need to have the utmost respect for people. We are all busy and some people just don't have the time to meet and that's OK, but you need to continue to build that network of trusted advisors. I mentioned how I have become friends with Tim Gannon who is the founder of Outback Steakhouse. Tim is a legend and such a good man with a fascinating story.

I met Tim first at the 2015 Necker Cup. We hit it off immediately and I was consumed by his stories and his love of Ireland. I actually gave him one of my Davis Cup jerseys which he still has today. Tim gave me his email address, I sent him an email and didn't get a response. I respect how busy he is but I sent him one or two emails after that with some things that he was interested in. I didn't pester him with emails and he would come back a little later but not all the time.

All of a sudden I got an email from him out of the blue about him getting an Irishman of the Year award from

The Ireland Funds and would I be one of his guests. I went to Palm Beach and stayed with him, we played tennis every day and now we are great friends. My point is I didn't overdo it contacting him but I stayed in the conversation. Relationships and building a network take time but it is worth it.

People would say to me I'm a good networker. I'm actually never too comfortable with that word because I think it sounds quite sleazy. However, your network is crucial in your career and it's important you build it; 60% of people's next job will come through networking, but it's generally something we don't train. I never want to be the person that when they see I'm calling they think oh no, what does James want this time? I think it comes down to having good EQ and putting yourself in someone else's shoes. I don't believe in messaging people for the sake of it.

One of my pet peeves in networking is if I introduce you to someone without asking the other person's permission first. This for me is a no and someone said that to me early on. We need to be careful with that. Ironically enough I got a message this week from someone casually saying 'Will you send me such and such business person's number?'. This business person is not the type of person who would give their number out to anyone. I sent this person a message letting them know that a specific person had asked for their number and was it OK for me to send on. They said it was but I wanted that permission first.

When It comes to networking I will always lead by being respectful, believing in people, adding value and being authentic.

You improve by being around good people

It's important in life to get yourself around good people. People who are positive and will build you up as opposed to knocking you down. You will notice that theme running throughout the book.

I love the quote from Oscar Wilde: "Be yourself, everyone else is already taken." This is very true. One of the ways I have been able to build a good network is to be authentic. I am myself and I tend not to get nervous around people. It's important that you are not someone you are not. I think successful people notice this.

It's funny sometimes when groups of business people come to Necker to see how nervous they can get around Richard. It's completely normal and I can see why. He is an icon of business. It's interesting to see these high-powered CEOs and founders looking like kids in a sweet shop. One junior executive I worked with would get nervous meeting an external senior business person. When I asked her why, she had these reasons around what would they talk to her about? And was she good enough to be there? People are people and I think we all grow in confidence over time but we need to put ourselves in these situations so we can develop.

When I was coaching on Necker I would host a tennis event every week on the island. It was fun but also a little bit stressful as you had lots of people wanting to play tennis and there are only two courts so you need to try and manage everything. I remember for one of the events a guest asked me to grip his racket. I said, "Yes no problem,

I just need to get these people out to play." Anyway he asked me again and I said yes. The person wasn't being rude but could possibly have asked at a more convenient time.

I remember a few hours later sitting with Richard and he asked me was this person giving me bother. I said no, that he asked me to put on a grip and the timing was wrong but it was fine. I remember thinking that one of Richard's strengths is that he saw that situation from afar and can read people. You need to be yourself because I believe that the vast majority of successful people will realise if you're not.

When I got to Necker, Josh Gilmour who was the coach said, "Richard comes down at 6am and you make him a cup of tea and have a chat and play." It sounds very stupid but I have barely drunk tea in my life and am conscious of how people like their tea and was quite nervous about making him a cup. I made him tea and he always said, "This is great," but I remember sitting with him and saying, "I never make tea so I'd say it would be best if you made your own." He loved it and my feeling around these types of people is you should be honest.

There is great value in chit chat. When I was on the tennis tour one of my nicknames was the King of Chit Chat. I would speak to anyone who would listen! I liked speaking to people on trains, buses, planes etc. I mentioned earlier about retiring from tennis and reaching out to people for coffee and advice. One of the best pieces of advice I got from a business person was to read the newspaper every day.

Their point was that if you meet someone from a certain industry then you need to be able to make conversation with them at a high level around their industry.

These people do not expect you to be an expert on their industry but you should be able to know what's going on at a high level. Every morning when I wake up I look at four or five online news sources to see what's happening. I remember working with an aircraft leasing company and being able to say I saw Boeing bought x amount of planes or something along those lines. Sometimes I find with sports or business people they can't move off their topic. You need to have various topics that you have knowledge of so you can navigate through.

Sometimes you need a dose of inspiration and getting around good people does it. I have mentioned how good the India training camp was for me and the opportunity to train with the best in the world and how that brought me on. I think from time to time we all need inspiration or we can become a little bit stale. Is there a conference that you can sign up for? Or can you take two days up a mountain to be inspired again? It can be unique to you but I always find it's important to put yourself around good people who will inspire you to be the best version of yourself.

CHAPTER 7

BEING AUTHENTIC

I believe that when it comes to performance and achieving your goals by yourself or a team then you have to be honest with both parties. Authenticity is key here. You can improve your chance of success by being authentic with yourself.

The truth is that sometimes the truth hurts. In a sport like tennis the rankings are the rankings. You can leave this book and google my results and see every pro or Davis Cup match I played. A professional rugby player said to me once, "We get judged once a week in a match." Sportspeople get judged by their results but so do business people. If you're in sales the company knows exactly what you have sold. It is all the same. You need to look at the data of how you're doing and be true to yourself. By being true to yourself it can help you move forward to achieve.

I remember one established pro tennis player said to me, "Players like the idea of hard work but actually don't work hard enough." Yes, the rankings don't lie but we need to put in the work to reach our goals. I think a lot of people like to create the illusion of 'hustling' to the top with posts across social media, but the bottom line is you need to work hard. I remember that match we played against Max Mirnyi in Davis Cup in Belarus. During the practice week Max was the first one there warming his body up long before the rest of the Belarus team arrived. You have to be willing to work hard. The same is true in business. The old saying was get into work early; sometimes people do that but it could just be to show the boss they are there and working even if they are not working. You have to put in the work and work smart.

You have to be clear on your vision and really want it. You need those honest conversations. My ranking was 145 and had stagnated a little bit. I wanted to be in the top 100 but if I'm honest with myself I probably burned out a little and didn't want to travel as much anymore. One thing that happens in sport, especially tennis, is that someone else wants it for you like maybe a parent. This is quite common. It's common in business too. I have worked with several high-performing teams where the manager wants to drive on the team and is obsessed with achieving, but some members of the team are comfortable with what they are doing and are just floating along. It depends who you want on your team and being comfortable with them.

I was lucky to have the most amazing person helping me financially the last few years in my career. His name is

Dan Grossman and he is also a great tennis player and has been number 1 in the world in the over 60s in doubles. He is a very successful businessman and a good friend. I have been very lucky to stay with him and his wife Cathy several times in San Francisco. When I let him know after that match in Italy that I would stop playing he said, "You will do great because you're a strong decision maker." I think you need to make these tough decisions.

I used to concern myself much more with what people thought of me. In tennis I used to wonder if someone thought I was good or bad or what they thought of my game. I had that imposter syndrome of sometimes not feeling good enough. I know now that this is normal but there were times I struggled with it. One thing I realised is that things just move on and deep down no one really cares too much as they are concerned with their own lives. When I stopped playing I remember thinking I would get loads of messages from people, which I did, but within a few days it's all forgotten and you think what am I going to do now?

The new tennis rankings come out and you're slowly sliding down them until you disappear. When I went into the corporate world I thought it was even more cut-throat. Someone announces they are leaving, you go for a team meal and in some cases that person is never spoken about again. My point is to be concerned with yourself and your own development and where you're going because everybody else will be fine.

When I played for LSU in college tennis I gave it everything I had for four years. They honour you on your senior day and want to stay connected to your success on the pro circuit, but the bottom line is out of sight and out of mind, the team moves on and you need to as well. I think you have to be loyal to people and it's a great quality in someone, but you also have to look after yourself as your company or team will do the same.

I remember working one to one with a retiring professional rugby player. He was making similar points about looking after yourself. He played for a certain team for a few years and went into the manager's office to discuss a transfer because he knew a bigger team was interested in signing him. He said the manager gave him a big speech on how they are a family and look at what we are building here etc. He said the manager was so passionate and convinced him to stay. A few months later the manager announced to the team that he was moving on because he got an offer he couldn't refuse. Be loyal but don't have blind loyalty either.

People see through bullshit

I believe with experience you get better at seeing through people's bull and sometimes you need to get burnt to learn some hard lessons.

This is where your network comes in. The world is a small place and I always think you're only one or two people removed from somebody. It's quite easy to speak to someone and find out about their reputation and character and if you want to do business with them. If someone approaches me about doing something specific and I don't know them well, I will most likely check LinkedIn and see who we are connected with. I will give my contact a call about the person to see if they are legit and trustworthy.

I host several tennis events a year and love bringing people together. It's all very casual with dinner after. I remember at one of the events there was a guy who is a hard salesman sitting beside someone I didn't want him next to. I didn't control where the people were sitting and I knew this person was getting the ear talked off him. I said it to him the next day. His point was that sometimes in business you are made to feel like you are being used. We all know the feeling when someone is speaking to us at an event but they are looking around for someone more important to speak to. Experienced business people see through this and you will too as you move throughout your career.

These days people use the internet and can google someone in five seconds to see if they are being genuine about their career and their past. One person I met in London was a tech founder who said all the right things. On the outside he drove a nice car and lived in a nice house and has spoken at events, and it seemed you couldn't meet a more legit person. I got burned a bit by him in a business setting and then moved off page one of Google to find other articles. What I found blew my mind. Ex-employees wrote an article about how this was an invisible company and it was all bull. He was swindling money from everywhere. I learned you have got to do your research to see through people.

The thing is that now it's so easy to do that research. Even think of something like Glassdoor. I can review companies and what employees said about the company. Do I take one review too hard? No, and I need to see a lot to really think the review is legit, but these platforms make it 'sesame street simple' for us to do our background research.

Nowadays everything we have done is traceable and all our past experiences and qualifications in sport and business are there for everyone to see. The internet is such a powerful tool that before doing business with someone or starting that dream job you can do your research so you have all the facts to make that tough decision and give yourself the best chance of being right.

People will believe in your vision

If you are authentic with yourself and your team then those people will believe in your vision. If you believe in it, it's almost contagious. I remember going into the office to meet Dave Mullins in Fitzwilliam. At the time Dave was the club manager. He was a former college and professional tennis player and very passionate about fitness and keeping active. I said to him I wanted to break the world record for the longest doubles match and he naturally asked how long it is. I said it's 57 hours but we can do it. I kind of thought we could do it but I went into the conversation enthusiastic about our chances and how I wanted him to be involved with it. I gave him the facts I had but I gave them in a positive way. Just to be clear, I didn't tell him any lies or fabrication but I told him the idea with passion. If you are passionate then you are looking to attract other passionate and good people to a project. You have to set yourself up for success.

I have mentioned a former coach of mine, Peter Clarke. The thing about Clarkey as he's known is he is the most positive man I've ever met. When he was coaching me I would walk on to a tennis court thinking I could beat anyone. He had this incredible positivity and power to make you feel good about yourself. However, I do think you also need to be realistic and he did venture sometimes into the unrealistic world. I remember Sunderland Football Club got promoted and the Irish midfield legend Roy Keane was the manager. They played Tottenham Hotspur away at White Hart Lane and won 1-0 with Michael Chopra scoring the only goal on the opening day of the season. I remember thinking wow what a result for a newly promoted team. Clarkey called me and said he thought Sunderland could win the league. When I said there was no chance, he went into this big rant about why not and what do I know etc. Now Sunderland didn't win the league and were average but Clarkey's positivity has stayed with me, but I do think you need a sprinkle of realism thrown in as well.

I have mentioned Dr Betty Uribe earlier in the book. She is one of the people who has been amazing to me. She has been a great mentor and friend. She is always helping me with speaking performances or getting me involved in what she's doing. Always connecting me with great people and an incredible person. Her attitude and positivity is something else. In the early days I would have said, "Dr Betty I can't do that," but her attitude is always, "Well why not?" She has been working against the odds her whole life growing up in Colombia and being an entrepreneur and rising to the top of California Bank. She has done it by being positive and delivering.

I'm sure some people reading this book will have kids or volunteer with sports teams etc. It's amazing what impact you can have on a kid's life. My junior tennis coach Larry Jurovich had such an impact on my journey. In Ireland at the time it was about winning Irish tournaments and being number 1 there. What he did was raise our expectations in an authentic way. He raised our standards. We truly had a high-performance squad with each player pushing each other. Larry was super positive and believed in me and the others but he also was realistic and looked at the facts. Early on we didn't believe in ourselves but by him stating his belief in us we raised our expectations. Show belief in your team in work or your local team as that belief will be contagious.

The truth is that times have changed for people. People want to be around positive and good people. People are not going to stay in a company where the boss shouts or bullies or the company doesn't look after employees. They will walk down the street and get a job somewhere else. I think of our parents' generation where typically you would get a job and stay there for 50 years and then get a nice watch as a gift at the end. It doesn't work like that. It's hard for a leader to get the best out of people if he or she is being negative with their team.

While I was on Necker I was sitting by the tennis courts one day having a cup of tea when an older woman came and sat down. Her name was Jill and her daughter was working on the island. She said to me, "How are you getting on with Richard?" I said great, that I was having a good time and learning lots. She then went on to tell me how she was one of the first air stewardesses with Virgin Atlantic. Richard has written publicly about carrying a notebook in his back pocket. Jill said that he would get on the plane and go to each Virgin employee with his notebook and ask them how they could improve the company. People want to feel valued and listened to. They will not stay if it's not a good environment to work in.

I strongly believe that as business moves forward people want to be part of a mission. They want to be part of something unique and something that's good for humanity. I strongly believe that. Capitalism is changing and companies need to absolutely focus on making good returns for their shareholders but also doing something good for the world, starting with their own people. We have all seen, felt and read the issues around climate change. Capitalism has to be a force for good in helping to solve the world's problems. I think there's been a shift and people want to be a part of something bigger than themselves and have a positive impact on the world around them.

When we were attempting the Guinness World Record Dave devised a plan around five-minute breaks and timings etc. He presented the plan to the players and Leo our trainer, and we gave some small input and changes, but the plan stayed pretty much the same. However, when we saw the plan I thought wow now this seems a lot more achievable. Take a day or two for an offsite with your company and discuss the plan, make them feel involved and get buy-in from the group on the direction you're going.

Our shining light for the whole Guinness World Record was Leo Daniel who looked after us in terms of nutrition and training. He had an individual plan for each of us based on our body types and what we should be eating and not eating. Again by presenting this plan to us he gave us confidence that we could go and break the record. As always it's important to note that things will go wrong and they did. Sometimes we didn't eat the exact piece of food that Leo asked us to but we had the framework there to go and break the record.

Granted, I am biased because I run offsites for teams, but there's so much to be said for getting the group into the room to address key issues. Sometimes we are just busy being busy and chasing stuff. There's tension on a wider team working in different departments and it's crucial to get everyone together for a time to give them some input, but present to them the vision so you get significant buy-in from the group. Nothing is ever going to be perfect but you need to set yourself up for success and including the group is a good way to do this.

CHAPTER 8

FOCUSING ON YOUR OWN AGENDA

Sometimes I feel I contradict myself because on one hand I absolutely love people and believe strongly you need to work with people to succeed, but on the other hand people work off their own agenda and people will do stuff when it suits themselves.

People can be a distraction

I have spoken throughout the chapters about my belief in getting around good people. However, people are great but they can also distract you from your goals. That's why your vision as an individual or being on a team is so important. If you are not clear on your vision you will lose focus on your goal. I have had to navigate this and feel like

I still struggle with it. I see myself as a good person and open to ideas and listening to people. People will come to me and ask me to get involved in something, either a business opportunity or maybe sit on a board. At times these absolutely make sense but I think at other times it just drags you away from your vision.

I was fascinated by Chris and Crystal Sacca after spending a week with them on Necker. I thought they were very interesting and fun people to hang out with. They make a great team. After meeting them I started researching and watching some interviews with Chris around investing. One point he made wasn't about investing but made a lot of sense to me for individuals hungry for success as entrepreneurs or on high-performance teams. He said to get off email. Sounds crazy but the point he made was yes have a slot to check email between certain times but other than that be working. He made the point that if you sit on email all day you are on someone else's agenda and not your own. Get back on your own agenda.

Keep the focus

You have to focus on your goals and vision and not be distracted in going to achieve that vision. It happens all the time in sport. The hot prospect pro player goes off the rails and ends up in pubs or clubs every night and doesn't dedicate himself/herself to their sport. In business you have someone with great potential but they easily get distracted and just can't seem to execute on the goals. It's down to you on what you want to achieve but you need to focus in order to be successful.

I attended lots of business events in the last few years. I have met some amazing people but have also met a lot of people that will try and leverage your contacts. I always look for common ground with someone and look to find out what their interests are outside of work and discuss those before discussing what we could do together. I went to an event with someone from a certain company once and the next day I went to the office with them. The first thing their manager said was, "Who did you meet? Any good contacts?" and grilled the individual around it. This is not the way to approach events. The key to building a good network is to give value. How can you help someone?

The title of the chapter is focusing on your own agenda as well and this is crucial. In terms of events I would always get a list of attendees and highlight two or three key people I would like to meet. I generally like to go to networking events alone because it ensures you have to speak to someone. I went to one professional services event where a lot of the company's staff were there. They literally stayed in the corner and spoke to each other. I will look for the key people, go up and introduce myself and ask them questions about themselves. If it feels right I will ask them for their contact details. I never feel the need to force it though and it has to be natural. People can distract you and there are users out there, but you need to focus on your own agenda and when you go to an event be purposeful and meet the people you need to meet.

Achieving your goals is tough and if it was easy everyone would do it. There is no substitute for hard work, you simply have to put the work and effort in, trust the plan and good things will happen. When Richard Branson was coming to Dublin for a speaking engagement he asked me to play tennis with him. From spending time with Richard I know how hard he works and how much fun he has doing it and this was the first time I was with him overseas. He was flying in from the States and landing at 5.30am. His Dublin day consisted of him going to the hotel and having something light to eat at 6.00am, then coming to play tennis with me from 7-8.00am then off to speak at a Virgin Media event, off to open a climate change project, a business lunch, then on stage for a few hours at the event and straight to the hotel for the event dinner where he said a few words, and then to the airport and out. I mean, that is some serious work ethic. It's always so impressive to see how dedicated he is to his physical fitness. It would never not be in his diary.

Work ethic is crucial

To be the best you have to put in the work. I mentioned the legendary former world number 1 tennis player Max Mirnyi who was nicknamed The Beast. His status on the tour for work rate is legendary. We played Davis Cup against Belarus for a second time and this time it was in Dublin. We lost the tie to the better team and both teams were in the same hotel. On the Sunday of a Davis Cup tie and if we didn't have a tournament the following week, the team would always go out for dinner and a few drinks if people wanted. It's important to socialise. I remember this specific Sunday leaving my room at 7pm to go and meet the others. The gym happened to be on my floor and I met The Beast Max in his tennis gear. He gave me a big smile and said, "Have a great night." He would never be outworked.

One of my heroes is golfer Padraig Harrington. He's from Dublin and sadly I've never met him, but hopefully one day I will get to have a coffee with him. You can watch all the pump videos you want but my favourite is the one for Padraig on YouTube. It starts with an interview on the course after he won the British Open. Tears not rolling down his eyes and he says, "You know I'm a worker, I'm a worker." He has won three golf majors in his career including the Open Championship twice in 2007 and 2008 and the PGA Championship in 2008.

I remember listening to an interview with him in Ireland in 2015 where he had won his first tournament in seven years at the Honda Classic. They said something to the effect that he was obviously getting older and was he slowing down at all. He replied, "Well I'll be home on Monday and will hit x amount of puts and drives Monday, Tuesday, Wednesday etc. Do you think I'm slowing down?" It's that attention to detail and work rate that he has in spades. Some people want to achieve their goals. If they were being truthful with themselves they would actually say they don't really mind. You have to really want to achieve your goals.

You must keep the focus and try not to get disheartened. Believe in that vision and go after it. When I was a junior I wanted to be number 1 in Ireland, go to college in the States, play Davis Cup, play Wimbledon and be in the top 100. I was lucky to achieve a few of those goals and missed some others. As Buffet and Gates said, focus is key. I remember early on my coach-player relationship with Larry Jurovich. He said to our squad, "I was a good hockey player and I think I could have been great but I found alcohol and women." That's what happens when people get disheartened in corporate life or in sport; they lose focus and turn to other things. Don't fall into that trap. Refocus and go again.

I remember being 16 years old which is a time when most Irish teens are out with their friends having some drinks. It's quite common in Ireland. I was a shy kid and was really the tennis guy in school and largely kept to myself. However, I was very comfortable in the tennis environment in Dublin, I had friends and I was very happy. It's amazing how big an impact a mentor/coach can have on you. Larry really looked after our group and turned us against the nights out and drinks. Now you might say would you not go out and have fun? We did have fun and that was on the tennis court. I remember my dad who is a traditional Irishman asking why I wasn't going out for drinks. The truth is I was focused on my goals and was obsessed with tennis. If you want to achieve then you must have balance, but you must focus.

We have spoken about the importance of the vision and what you are trying to achieve. It's important whether you are in corporate life or not that you create your own vision and have people support you in achieving that vision. Sport is the easiest example for this. Too many times parents dictate their kids' vision and impose it on them and basically live life through them. I was lucky that my parents were incredibly supportive. They encouraged me when I needed a little push but it was my own vision. I have seen countless times where parents live through their kids and the kid ends up quitting sport at a young age and never playing again.

This vision imposing is common in business and obviously a little more tricky to deal with. Someone might come into a team. In a team people want to feel understood and listened to and you need to give them that feeling of being listened to and valued. As an individual going after your vision is difficult. The question to ask yourself is to look in the mirror and really decide is this what I want to achieve? If it isn't then that's fine and do what you like. Kurt and Teresa Long are champions of creating that vision. In their eyes the vision and the mission are the most important things and then hiring the best people around you to help you achieve that vision, or if it's your personal life then getting the best support network around you.

David McKiernan who is the founder of Java Republic epitomises what you can do having a strong vision. He started Java Republic in 1999 and built the brand from the ground up. In my opinion Dave did this by having a passion for his business, never giving up even when times were tough and going after this vision with all his might. Sometimes you need a little bit of luck, but you can't help but be enthusiastic about life after spending time with Dave.

Another thing to be aware of is negative people can drag you down. It's important to get around good people and not stay around these negative folk. You can be polite with them but then move on. These people are jealous and wish they were as good as you. It's one thing to see someone's success and learn from it and it's another thing to be jealous about it. I don't know if I've ever had a jealous streak when it came to business. I'm competitive and am eager to learn from people but it's never gone into jealousy. I believe in treating people with respect and trying to help people. I believe in serendipity and how it comes back around, but I have learned a hard lesson and am much more protective of my network.

You need to watch your own jealousy, recognise it, acknowledge it and move on. When I was under 18 I would have been jealous of another Irish player doing well and be envious of their performance. I recognised this and began to approach it in a different way. In Chapter 1 I mentioned UCLA basketball coach John Wooden. Anytime I feel myself getting jealous of someone else's achievements I think of Wooden's quote on success: "Success is peace of mind which is a direct result of self-satisfaction in knowing you made the effort to become the best you could." Success is not you trying to beat someone else, it's around you being the best version of yourself. Success means different things to different people, and as an individual and leader you need to recognise that.

Another thing about being around negative people is to recognise that they don't have the same mindset as you. They are not as driven as you are. When I started HC

Collective some people said to me, "What are you doing? Just stay in a normal job and work your way up." My attitude is that life is short and you need to be able to pay your bills and have fun doing what you're doing. I knew I could add value to people in what I was doing and I wanted to see if I could make a business out of it. Luckily I'm doing OK and happier career wise than I ever was since my pro tennis days.

When I first thought about going after the Guinness World Record I knew I had to approach a certain type of person. Someone who might not necessarily say yes but would be at least positive about it. You know the people in your network that are positive and approachable. You need to gravitate towards them. Make a list of the positive people in your life and try to distance yourself from the negative people. I know there are certain interactions with not nice people that you have to have. That is life but it's important to seek out positive people with the same mindset as you because you're more likely to be successful.

The other thing to realise is that some people are content doing the same job and floating along through life. That is absolutely fine and people should do whatever makes them happy. Sometimes I see that in places like the Caribbean. The people are so relaxed, friendly and happy and a lot of them are very content doing the same job through life and floating along. There is absolutely nothing wrong with that. It's up to you to decide what will make you content. I guess that by reading this book you are hoping for more than this.

You need to be aware that people can be intimidated by you. You stand out and they know it. They know how good you are. People can turn to sly comments or even bullying. This is very challenging for someone to deal with, but it's based around their own insecurities more than anything you have or haven't done. My attitude to these people is to almost feel sorry for them and not let these comments or remarks get you down. There really is no point in this.

One of the female leaders I have spent time with shared her experience of working in a male-dominated industry and the issues she had to deal with. She feels the men were intimidated by her, were jealous and simply did not have the right mentality. It's something that I can't say I have any experience of; however, I believe you can absolutely address the issues with someone but you also need to be confident in yourself and continue to strive for your goals.

CHAPTER 9

WORKING WITH PEOPLE

To achieve your goals you are going to have to work with a team of people effectively. Working in siloes is lonely. A lot of the time when I work with organisations I see that many people end up working in siloes on their own. It's important to bring these people back and make them feel part of the team. The truth is that the majority of people want to be on a team but sometimes we drift away. There has obviously been a major shift towards remote working. Remote working is great and absolutely should be encouraged but you can't beat getting people in a room. This is not possible at the moment with the coronavirus but I believe it will be possible again in the future.

The best teams that I was a part of in college at LSU was when we had a strong team culture. When the team spent time together with each other outside of practice and people bought into that culture. Yes you want to have a competitive culture but you also need to have fun. In corporate life the highest performing teams I see are the ones that do something outside work together from time to time or play games for fun on occasion in the office. I'm not saying you need to do something every week but you do need times where people can let their guard down and have fun together.

Build a strong culture

Larry built that performance culture in my junior days. The interesting thing about tennis is it's an individual sport yet you can still have that bond where people are competitive and pushing each other to be better. It's common in hard sales organisations where team members don't get on and are not really working together. It's important to foster an environment where these people at least take shared learnings and best practice so they have the best chance in succeeding to hit their targets. In tennis you are competitive and trying to move your ranking up, but other players will share most of the time tactically how they think you can beat someone.

On the tour my favourite doubles partner was French player Fabrice Martin. We remain great friends and we clicked as a team on the court but especially off the court. Fabrice has gone on to make the final of the French Open in doubles and is currently ranked 24 in the world. One thing about Fabrice is he never gets flustered and he has an ability to adapt and get on with different doubles partners and play well with them. The best doubles players have that ability to get the best out of themselves and also bring the best out in others. Fabrice does that.

It's essential to get around good people. I can't stress this enough. "Surround yourself with the people you want to become." You need to go and find a group of people or a team that you bring value to but that also add value to you. I have mentioned going to India to train with the best in the world. Is there a team you can support and learn from? A lot of the time people are too afraid to ask. What's the worst thing that can happen? Someone will say no. You need to put yourself on a high-performance team if you are not on one if you want to continue to develop. This has been and continues to be my philosophy. I have made mistakes along the way but I have met some amazing people.

It's almost like finding your tribe. Get involved in things that interest you and you will meet like-minded people. You also need to note that it is important to meet people outside your tribe too. I think tennis has been very kind to me on this front. I have been a member of Fitzwilliam Lawn Tennis Club since I was 14 after I was offered membership for doing well in the juniors. The club has been great to me in terms of tennis but also meeting like-minded people and that network of people helped me transition into business.

In London I have some friends that are members of the All England Club at Wimbledon. It's the most special tennis club in the world and on the site where the Wimbledon Championships are played. Every time I meet my friends Johnny Barr and Ashley Tatum at the club you can tell how proud they are of the place and there is the ultimate community feeling there where everyone knows each other and is active in the club. Find your tribe whatever that might be.

I have been doing some speaking on high performance and goal setting which I am very much enjoying. When I was preparing for my first talk it made me think of my own journey. When I was 18 and looking at US colleges I was torn between signing for Indiana or Louisiana State University. Indiana was ranked 60 in the country and based in beautiful Bloomington Indiana. One of my best friends from Ireland was in the team and I knew if I signed there I would have an instant friend and be one of the best players in the team. It was also indoor tennis there which would suit my game.

My other option was to go to LSU. They were ranked 10 in the country and it was outdoors in 40 degree heat every day. I would be fighting for my place in the team in the first year and really had to prove I was good enough. I was torn between the two, but deep down I knew that LSU was the better place for my tennis development and I went there. I think life is about decisions and we make some good and some bad, but a key is to do your best to get around good people and push yourself on.

When I go to events that are of interest to me, if I like the speaker I will always go up at the end and speak to them and say thanks for speaking and that I very much enjoyed their talk because of x and y. More often than not a speaker will say, "Connect with me on LinkedIn" or "here's my card." You need to put yourself in these situations to meet people you want to meet.

I love the story of Roger Bannister and the four-minute mile. People said it was impossible to run a mile in under four minutes. You might collapse and die and medically it is impossible. Roger Bannister broke the four-minute mile on 6 May 1954 and ran it in a time of three minutes and 59.4 seconds. Within a year of Bannister breaking the four-minute mile record three runners broke it in a single race.

Success comes with the help of others. You need to work with others to achieve. Doing it alone is lonely and not that much fun really. Dr Betty who I mentioned is a big fan of this. She believes in working together and standing alongside people to achieve. I think there are too many times where we just don't want to ask for help. We need to ask and get support when we need it. We see that in society with mental health issues. It's not weakness to go and speak to someone about the challenges you are facing and if anything it shows great strength. There is no I in team and it's tough to succeed alone.

When you are in a team you must do your absolute best to leverage your team's strength. People have strengths and there has to be a reason they are in the team, and you need to leverage that person's expertise and knowledge. When we did the Guinness World Record I specifically said to Dave we had to get a good trainer and to do it properly. Leo was perfect for this as he had knowledge around the key areas that we needed and we trusted him to support us with it. I can write this and say I don't think we would have broken the Guinness World Record without Leo. His name is not in the book but it should be.

I loved reading the Airbnb story of how Brian Chesky co-founded the company and how when they looked to raise money people thought it was a crazy idea. At the time it was and one high-profile investor predicted there would be a murder in an Airbnb early on and the business would be over. How wrong was that person! When it comes to teams I enjoyed watching an interview with Reid Hoffman who is a co-founder of LinkedIn and Brian Chesky of Airbnb. Chesky is obsessed with hiring the right people and personally interviewed the first few hundred employees. When it comes to a team it's important you have the right people with the right strengths and you can leverage those strengths.

The truth of life is that in a team of say 15 people there will be personality clashes along the way. You need to manage those situations and keep the team going in the right direction. One business leader of a tech company gave me the brutal truth that if they don't get on with other people in the team then they had better be exceptional performers. This might sound wrong but it's actually right. I think of Eric Cantona at Manchester United in the late 1990s. He was causing trouble off the pitch but Ferguson knew how important he was to the team and there were almost different rules for him than there were for others. There is a fine line here but as long as the ship is moving forward you need to keep going with it.

You need to take notice of quiet team members. Sometimes quiet team members offer the most value. I have found that when I work with companies for offsites and I do my sit down one to one with the team members it is often the quiet team member that has the most powerful thing to say. Sometimes in a team offsite there's that person that can take over the room and not let others speak. It is the facilitator's responsibility to get that key information from the quiet person. Just because someone is quiet it doesn't mean they have nothing to say. Very often they have more to say than you think. An Indian tribe leader usually speaks last.

I always found that with Richard Branson too. He is actually quite quiet but is a very good listener. He lets people speak before he says anything and you can see he is taking it all in. I mentioned Ray Nolan who is a serial entrepreneur and has sold several companies. I asked Ray if I could sit in with him in a meeting and learn from him. I went into his office and found the experience fascinating. He actually didn't say much and let the other guy almost talk himself out. The guy was a marketing person and was going on and on. Ray was quiet but then made his points clearly and concisely. Sometimes people talk too much and we need to get to the point in a respectful polite way, but the key is to be a good listener.

You must leverage your team's strength because they might cover your weakness. In my professional tennis days I was primarily playing doubles. When looking for a doubles partner I would think how this person is plugging my weaknesses, and with our strengths and weaknesses combined do we make a strong team? In business or life find people that plug your weaknesses and overall make you a better person.

That was obvious to me with several people including the founders of Voxpro, Dan and Linda Kiely. Their strengths and weaknesses match together like none other and they make a great team. If you are an entrepreneur can you get a details person to help you execute the parts of the business that aren't going well or that you're not strong at? One of my favourite books is *Principles* by billionaire investor Ray Dalio. He is a massive fan of personality tests and understanding your people. The strength of getting people working together on projects effectively, matching people's strengths with other people's weaknesses.

You need to recognise that having disagreement in a high-performing team can be a good thing if it's done in a respectful way. It shows the rest of the team you care. I was never afraid to go to the coach at LSU and argue for myself or someone to play in a certain team spot. You did things for the good of the team but you could disagree. In college tennis there are three doubles matches going on. My last year of college I dropped down to play number 3 because we needed some experience to get the doubles point and we were strong at the top. I wasn't happy with the decision but when I went to the coach and made my case and he made his we both agreed that he was right and I played there. It's good to have disagreements but you need to do what's good for the team.

You can never be afraid to speak your mind. I'm a fan of former Manchester United and Ireland captain Roy Keane. He has never been afraid to speak his mind. His downfall over the years was probably he didn't always do it in a respectful way. It is important that you are measured in your comments. It is essential to take a step back from the situation and not jump in with anger as you will most likely say something you regret. In a team if someone says something you absolutely don't agree with then take four or five seconds breath and then make your point.

Disagreement in a team indicates honesty. I worked with a financial services company in the UK where there were heated discussions, but it was obvious there was sheer honesty in the room and people were saying things not to be controversial but to help the team move forward. You need to get to a place in a team where these conversations can happen. They are most likely going to happen outside of the working office environment and somewhere a little more casual.

Sometimes everything isn't great and it needs to be said. There's an element where people can be overly positive, and if things are terrible then it needs to be said and addressed how you move forward from this point. You are where you are. It will be a relief to people and everyone will be thinking it, but it needs a leader to say it. The theme of the book is to be positive, but I said earlier the facts don't lie and if things are bad then we need to take a step back, readjust the plan and go again.

During the Guinness World Record Luke was the freshest one of us all. He is a smart kid and very relaxed about things but he is never afraid to speak his mind. When Dan was struggling with his body Luke would say it and he wouldn't dance around the issue. You need these people in your team that have a sense of realism when it comes to performance and what exactly is going on.

Having disagreements in a team is pushing the team forward. In one corporate I worked with the team wasn't being pushed forward because they knew that whatever they said was not listened to. The key is that the information is taken and used in a positive way to help move the team forward.

CONCLUSION

It has been a goal of mine to write a book but I wasn't sure if I could actually do it. I think if I sent this to my English teacher from school he would be in shock. I did have a clear vision but I'm still a little surprised that I've made it to the end! I hope you will agree that I have had an interesting journey in tennis from picking up a racket in Swords tennis club at six years old to going right the way through to playing college tennis at LSU, playing professional tennis, holding a Guinness World Record and meeting and spending time with some of the most incredible entrepreneurs and business people in the world.

One of the things I get asked a lot is if I was a successful tennis player. My ranking was 145 in the world in doubles which doesn't set the world on fire. However, I'm content because I believe I got to about the highest ranking I could get to. Success is all relative and I would ask you what is success for you? What do you want to achieve? Once you do your absolute best then that's all you can do.

Over the course of the book I've shared with you some of the key lessons that I have learned in professional sport and business, both my own learnings and from other people. We all have our successes and failures and I've never claimed to have achieved every goal I've ever set out to, but I've always tried my best. It's amazing to think where my tennis racket has taken me. For me success with this book is my hope that you will take lessons and use them to help create and achieve your vision.

Life can be difficult at times and we all make mistakes along the way. All we can do is our absolute best and keep learning from our mistakes and pitfalls. We need to surround ourselves in both our personal life and business life with people that understand our shortcomings but want to work with us and support us with our goals. In turn we need to support them with their goals. Sometimes we fall down on this but we need to learn and keep moving forward.

This is the type of book that you can dip in and out of and read on several occasions. You really need to take your time and get clear on your vision and go after your goal. I have given you my cornerstone beliefs about how you will be successful and now it's up to you to go out and deliver on this.

One theme running through this book which I would like to emphasise is the importance of people and how we all need help and mentors through our life. Reach out to people and don't be afraid to ask for help. Through my journey you can see how much support I have had from some amazing people and this works the other way: we need to return the favour and help and mentor other people too.

You could just read this book and put it back on the shelf or you could take action and go after your goals. I hope you got as much enjoyment out of reading this book as I got writing it.

ABOUT THE AUTHOR

James Cluskey is a former professional tennis player ranked 145 in the world in doubles, Irish Davis Cup player, Guinness World Record holder and founder of HC Collective.

HC Collective works with individuals and organisations around high performance. They work one to one with people, both in person and remotely, looking to reach the next level, with corporate teams looking to work together more effectively. James also gives keynotes on the topics of high performance, networking and career transition.

James is from Dublin, Ireland and is fascinated by all things sport. He continues to play tennis regularly, loves to play paddle tennis and is a huge fan of hiking.